INSIGHT COMPACT GUIDES

Washin...

CW00327113

Compact Guide: Washington, D.C. is a culture-based guide for a culture-based destination, revealing the splendors of the city's monuments, the wealth of its museums, and the delights of its streets and squares.

This is one of more than 80 titles in *Apa Publications'* new series of pocket-sized, easy-to-use guidebooks intended for the independent-minded traveler. *Compact Guides* are in essence travel encyclopedias in miniature, designed to be comprehensive yet portable, as well as up-to-date and authoritative.

Star Attractions

An instant reference to some of Washington's top attractions to help you set your priorities.

U.S. Capitol p16

National Gallery of Art p22

National Air and Space Museum p27

Lincoln Memorial p30

Vietnam Veterans' Memorial p31

White House p38

Georgetown pp47–52

Washington National Cathedral p57

Mount Vernon p64

National Zoological Park p59

Arlington National Cemetery p61

Washington, D.C.

Introduction

Places

Culture

Leisure

Practical Information

Washington, D.C. – America's Capital City

A visit to the capital city of the United States is nothing less than a grand lesson in history. In many respects it's living history since we are following in the very footsteps of the men and women who created the republic. In addition to the history, Washington also has a unique beauty. The real credit for that should go to the first American president, George Washington, who played a major part in the city's design.

Washington insisted on creating an entirely new city for the capital. To maintain the independence of the federal government from the influence of the various state governments, the city would have to be a separate judicial entity, subject only to the authority of the federal government. Its location on the Potomac River was chosen because of its central position between the northern states and the southern states, whose sectional strife was already making itself felt. But it was also a spot favored by President Washington himself. His home in Mount Vernon was only 15 miles (24km) downriver from the area.

George Washington

In 1790, a diamond-shaped area – exactly 10 miles (16km) on each side – between the Potomac and Anacostia rivers became the site for the capital of the United States. The land was taken partially from Maryland and partially from Virginia, and called the District of Columbia. (These days, locals call it simply "the District".)

Potomac River, from the terrace of the Kennedy Center 5

President Washington felt it was important to make the city as grand as Paris or London, or indeed, ancient Rome. To his assistance came a young French architect, Pierre Charles L'Enfant. The area of the city was surveyed by Andrew Ellicott and a free black man, Benjamin Banneker, a largely self-educated mathematician and scientist.

L'Enfant envisioned two major axes for his grand design. He chose the highest point, Jenkins Hill ("a pedestal waiting for a monument"), as the site of the Capitol building. Heading west from the foot of the Capitol there would be a grand avenue all the way down to the edge of the Potomac, where a monument to George Washington would stand. Perpendicular to that first axis at the monument, he would create another major artery, going from the monument to the site of the president's official residence.

Over the north–south, east–west grid of streets, L'Enfant superimposed radiating diagonal avenues leading to focal points (the innumerable traffic circles of today) – reminiscent of Paris.

L'Enfant's city was often characterized as a "city of magnificent distances" (even more "magnificent" in those days when there were hardly any buildings). Although the city is now graced with

a modern subway system, the Metrorail, visitors would do well to bring with them a good pair of walking shoes merely to cover those distances comfortably.

L'Enfant's plan was only partially realized during his lifetime, however. That grand avenue between the Capitol and the Washington Monument was for a long time an unkempt forest. Until the end of the Civil War, Washington was largely a sleepy, southern town with muddy or alternately, dusty, unpaved streets.

This started to change with the affluence of the late 19th century. The 1901 McMillan Plan for Washington, D.C. proposed a return to the grandeur of L'Enfant's vision if not to its details. The grand avenue sketched by L'Enfant would become a great park area, the Mall. A series of landfills on the Potomac River would create the new West and East Potomac Parks on which the Lincoln, the Vietnam Veterans', and the FDR memorials would be built. And a new railroad station in classic Beaux Arts style was built away from the Mall – Union Station.

Union Station

Later, a third renovation, called for by President Kennedy in 1961, would turn Pennsylvania Avenue into the ceremonial avenue that it was originally meant to be.

The beauty of official Washington is in stark contrast to much of the rest of the city, which is immersed in poverty and urban blight. Go only a few blocks from the Capitol and you start to find yourself in an increasingly impoverished, predominantly black city. In a sense, Washington is two cities – official Washington, largely in the northwest quadrant, and the rest of the city, still plagued by poverty, disease, and crime.

Location and Size

Washington is no longer exactly the 100 sq miles (260 sq km) authorized in 1790. The Virginia portion of the Dis-

Jogging on the Mall

trict was returned to its home state in 1846. Today, there-fore, the Potomac River serves as one of the boundaries of the District. Although Washington is technically a south-ern city, in cultural matters it maintains a healthy rivalry with New York, 252 miles (405km) north. There are good train, bus, and air connections between the two cities.

Local Geography

L'Enfant's plan divided the city into four quadrants (North-west, Northeast, Southwest, Southeast). Streets radiate out from the Capitol, designated by letters or numbers. Let-tered streets (A, B etc.) go east–west; numbered ones (First Street, Second Street) go north–south. Bear in mind that "First Street, N.W." (northwest of the Capitol) does not connect with "First Street, S.E." (southeast of the Capi-tol). Avenues are named after states, and cross this grid pattern at confusing angles.

Washington maintains an enviable system of parks and green areas. If you walked down Rock Creek Park from the Maryland border through the center of the District, you'd hardly notice you were in a city at all.

Climate

Politics aside, Washington's location is hardly ideal for a capital. In the days before air-conditioning, many foreign diplomats assigned to the U.S. mission would receive hard-ship pay, at least during the midst of summer when it is very hot – often above 90°F (32°C) – and very humid.

The winters are generally mild, but there are exceptions – and extreme ones at that. Severe snow storms occur in some years, and the city is inevitably ill-prepared for the consequences.

The best time to visit is during the spring (April to late June) or in the fall (September and October). If you come in spring, be prepared for the crowds, as the nation's cap-ital is a prime destination for schools. Cherry Blossom Week (usually early April, see page 33) is the most crowded. Around 20 million tourists come to Washington each year.

Visitors in summer
Tourists by the White House

The Federal Government

The federal government has three branches: the legisla-tive, executive, and judicial. To some extent, each is able to limit the powers of the other two.

Legislative power is vested in Congress, which con-sists of two bodies, the House of Representatives and the Senate. Both are elected directly by the people and act according to majority vote. They are organized into committees, which write, consider, and amend "bills" (new laws).

The House has 435 members; seats are allocated to each state in proportion to its population. House mem-

bers are elected for two-year terms. The House is led by the Speaker, elected by a majority of the members and therefore leader of the majority party. Bills can be introduced in either body of Congress, but only the House can initiate the spending of tax dollars, the real business of policies.

Statue of President Garfield by the Capitol

The Senate is considered the senior body of Congress. Senators represent entire states and are elected to six-year terms. Each of the 50 states, regardless of size, has two Senators. The Senate is nominally run by the Vice President of the United States. But the Vice President's power in the Senate is limited to voting only when there is a 50/50 tie.

When a bill is approved by both bodies of Congress, it is sent to the President, who can either sign it into law or veto it. Congress can override a presidential veto, if it can get a two-thirds majority in both the House and Senate in support of the bill.

Executive power resides in the presidency. Presidential and vice-presidential candidates always run for election as a team. They are the only officials elected by a vote of the entire population of the country. Presidents and vice-presidents are limited to four-year terms, and each can be re-elected only once for a total of eight years in office.

The president takes an active role in foreign policy, including the negotiation of treaties, and is Commander-in-Chief of the Armed Forces. The Congress, however, must ratify the treaties and has the power to declare war.

The executive branch of government is responsible for enforcing laws and implementing legislation. The president appoints members of the Cabinet, who direct the executive departments such as the Departments of State, Justice, Treasury, Agriculture, Labor, Commerce, Energy, and Transportation.

The third branch of the federal government is the Judiciary. The Supreme Court, the Appeals Courts, and the lower-level federal courts interpret the Constitution and the laws passed by Congress and the President. The court can invalidate a law by determining that it violates the Constitution.

Local Government

Washington, created to be the home of the three branches of the federal government, has always been under its direct supervision. The drawback is that the city's population has remained largely unrepresented. The District has only a non-voting delegate in the House of Representatives, and still has no senator. Local politicians have campaigned for years to make the District into the 51st state of the Union, but this is unlikely to happen in the near

Summer street-beat

future. Previously, the district was entirely under the thumb of the federal government, but with the success of the civil rights movement (the city's population being predominately black), it has achieved a certain degree of home rule. Washington now has an elected mayor and an elected city council.

People

The population of the District of Columbia is only slightly over 600,000, but when you include the Maryland and Virginia suburbs the figure rises to 4.6 million. There is a great turnover of population in Washington, especially when a new president takes office. But there are many people who find a permanent niche somewhere in the business of government. And then there are the people who didn't come here for political reasons, but who were born and bred in the area. A large percentage of these are African-Americans, who outnumber whites within the District.

The dream that the District of Columbia, as the nation's capital, would become a major commercial center was never fully realized. Washington was and remains a political town, with little industrial activity, and any benefits it may have received through the years have stemmed primarily from the political role it has played. With the great fortunes that moved into the city in the last quarter of the 19th century, little was created for the city, although the great mansions of the *nouveaux riches* have contributed to its architectural appeal.

The exclusive Cosmos Club on Massachusetts Avenue

One element that greatly affected the development of the city was the Civil War and the end of slavery. Congress outlawed slavery in the District of Columbia in 1862, sometime before President Lincoln issued his Emancipation Proclamation. Maryland and Virginia were still slave states, and slaves who managed to cross the boundary into the District automatically gained their freedom. Needless to say, hundreds of restless slaves came from Maryland's Prince George's and Montgomery counties across the Eastern Branch bridge to freedom.

When the Emancipation Proclamation came into effect in January 1863, the stream became a torrent. Freed slaves came on their own or, often enough, with the victorious Union armies, especially after Union troops led by General Sherman successfully saber-thrust into the South.

A Freedman's Village was set up near Arlington House that developed into a model miniature city, with houses, shops, a church, a school, a hospital, and a home for the aged. The colony became self-supporting. But many of the refugees took their chances in the city, which was soon dotted with poverty-stricken settlements of freed Negro slaves – with few jobs and little hope of employment.

Many went to work as laborers or signed on for naval duty. By the autumn of 1863, when the reluctance of many officers to accept Negro soldiers into the army had been largely overcome, many of the refugees were formed into units of the Union Army.

There was also a commitment among some Civil War veterans – black and white – to improve the living conditions of the black population. General Oliver Otis Howard had been the commissioner of the Freedman's Bureau and a strong proponent of a university for the growing black population of the city. When Howard University was created on March 2, 1867, by President Andrew Johnson, as an "institution for the training of preachers (colored) with a view to service among freedmen," it was with money raised by Howard's Freedman's Bureau.

Since then, the university has expanded. Howard has provided the civil rights movement with its lawyers, including Justice Thurgood Marshall, and today boasts of having produced more African-Americans with advanced degrees than any other institution.

Frederick Douglass, Afro-American orator

The area around LeDroit Park became a major center for a growing black middle class in the city, which remains an influential force in the African-American community nationwide. With the ebbs and flows of the economy, however, and almost total dependence of the city's working population on the federal government, Washington's black middle class has been fighting an uphill battle to alleviate the city's gnawing pockets of poverty and blight. As has often been the case in the black community, it has been the churches which have maintained a strong religious and cultural matrix for a population surrounded by poverty, disease, and crime.

Washington's unique position as a federal district, without representation in Congress for its citizens, has aggravated the situation. Black civil rights leaders in the District have therefore been striving for years to attain "home rule" for the District. Some political power has, indeed, been given to the District's voters, but the city's severe financial problems have led to calls in Congress for the District to be returned to total congressional control.

The Power Brokers

Meanwhile, across the city in the social whirl of Georgetown and Northwest Washington, the pace is somewhat different. Seldom is the flaunting of wealth as extravagant as it was in the heyday of the late 19th century, but the style has not changed much.

The parties, receptions, and social gatherings provide a means for reaching those compromises, making those deals, and establishing those contacts that make Washington work. The gala balls and state dinners at the White House are certainly the most prestigious events, but not necessarily the most important. Sometimes it's the more intimate gathering at a Foxhall Road estate of a small group of people making the right connections that really counts.

But politics today is much more public than previously, with all the major events covered by one of the C-Span cable television channels, which have a duty to broadcast all floor action in the Senate or the House of Representatives, or by CNN which concentrates on news programming.

Next to the Congress and the federal government officials, a considerable amount of influence in Washington lies on K Street, N.W., known by insiders as "Power Alley." This is where many of the law firms and lobby organizations, which represent industries and interest groups across the country, have their offices, from which they cultivate the needed contacts to influence policy.

Power brokers in action

The foreign diplomatic community in Washington also adds to the number of social gatherings, soirees, and dinner parties which the politically "savvy" people known to attend. Many of the embassies, in an effort to show off some of their local talent, organize concerts with some of their native artists, opera stars, or musicians.

Then there are the numerous "staffers," the non-elected officials who do the real nitty-gritty work in Congress or in the federal bureaucracy. Not limited by the need to get re-elected, they become something of a permanent civil service, sometimes wielding more power than the elected officials. They follow the issues closely. They make recommendations to the elected officials who often enough have so many items on their plate that they don't master any of them and are, therefore, totally reliant on their staff. If you feel strongly about an issue and want Congress to enact legislation which would benefit your cause, cultivating contacts with the appropriate staffers is the best way to expedite the process.

Historical Highlights

1608 English colonist Captain John Smith ventures up the Potomac River.

1751 Georgetown founded.

1789 Georgetown University founded by Bishop John Carroll.

1790 The first Congress, meeting in New York, decides that the new capital city will be located further south on the Potomac River.

1791 French-born architect Pierre Charles L'Enfant draws up plans for the capital city which "unite the useful with the commodious and agreeable."

1792 Construction begins on the White House, the first official building in the new city.

1793 George Washington lays the cornerstone of the new Capitol.

1797 Chain Bridge is built, the first to span the Potomac River.

1800 President John Adams occupies the still unfinished White House. His wife, Abigail, finds the rooms drafty, and uses the East Room as a drying room for the laundry. Library of Congress established with 3,000 books.

1807 First school for the city's black children set up by three black slaves.

1808 A curfew of 10pm is set for black residents.

1812 War of 1812 with Great Britain begins, after years of maritime trade disputes. A guidebook to the capital city is published.

1814 British troops set fire to the unfinished Capitol, White House and other public buildings. Heavy rain during the night prevents total devastation.

1820 Congress rejects city's request to ban slave trade from the District of Columbia.

1829 British gentleman-scientist and philanthropist, James Smithson, dies, leaving funds to establish the Smithsonian Institution.

1835 The "Snow Riots" erupt. White mobs are intent on maintaining slavery within the District of Columbia.

1846 Land originally taken from Virginia to create part of the District of Columbia is returned to the state.

1848 Work begins on the Washington Monument.

1853 Work begins on Washington Aqueduct which will bring much needed water from Great Falls to Georgetown and the District.

1861 Abraham Lincoln is inaugurated. Mayor of Washington refuses to take Union loyalty oath and is jailed.

1862 Congress outlaws slavery in the District; compensation paid to slave owners who swear allegiance to the Union.

1863 Lincoln's Emancipation Proclamation, a war measure which frees slaves in areas rebelling against the Union, takes effect. Capitol completed.

1864 Confederate forces under General Jubal Early approach the capital from Maryland, but are driven back.

1865 Lincoln's second inaugural ball held in the Patent Office. For the first time, blacks participate. Six weeks later, on April 14,

Lincoln is assassinated by John Wilkes Booth at Ford's Theater.

1866 Blacks get the vote in the District, several months before Constitution is amended to ensure their right to vote everywhere.

1867 District is granted territorial status, and Mayor Alexander "Boss" Shepherd embarks on a major public works program to improve conditions in the city.

1870 District of Columbia City Council bans racial discrimination in venues such as hotels and restaurants.

1874 The District's territorial government is disbanded, accused of corruption. Control over the District of Columbia returns to Congress. Father Patrick Healy named head of Georgetown University – the first black man to direct a large U.S. university.

1875 Congress passes Civil Rights Act, which outlaws segregation in theaters, places of worship, and cemeteries.

1877 Black leader Frederick Douglass is appointed Marshal of the District and Recorder of Deeds

1878 President and Mrs. Rutherford B. Hayes invite local children to roll Easter eggs on the White House lawn – starting an annual tradition.

1897 The Jefferson Building of the Library of Congress is completed. Work completed on land reclamation of the Potomac Flats, creating the new ground for West and East Potomac Parks.

1900 Centennial celebrations for the founding of City of Washington.

1901 A Congressional committee proposes the development of the city's park system.

1912 Griffith Stadium dedicated. President William Howard Taft opens the first baseball game by throwing out the first ball.

1924 Ku Klux Klan, the racist organization, conducts a parade to the Washington Monument.

1943 Pentagon completed.

1963 Civil rights march on Washington. The Reverend Dr. Martin Luther King, Jr. looks out over crowd of 200,000 at the Lincoln Memorial and says "I Have a Dream."

1967 New political structure for District of Columbia: a mayor appointed by Congress and an elected city council.

1968 Riots in Washington sparked by killing of Martin Luther King in Memphis, Tennessee. First presidential election since 1800 in which residents of District of Columbia are allowed to vote.

1971 For the first time in 100 years, Washington is allowed to elect a representative to Congress. Kennedy Center opens.

1972 Burglars break in to Democratic Party campaign offices at Watergate Hotel. They are linked to key figures in the Nixon White House.

1975 Congress allows District of Columbia to elect a mayor as well as city council.

1976 Metrorail service starts.

1982 Vietnam Veterans' Memorial completed.

1988 Restaurants and shops open at restored Union Station.

1995 Access to Pennsylvania Avenue in front of the White House restricted for security reasons.

1996 The city government's financial difficulties lead to increasing budgetary controls by Congress.

The Capitol Rotunda
Previous pages: The Capitol
with its reflecting pool

Tour 1

Capitol Hill

The Capitol – Supreme Court – Library of Congress – Folger Shakespeare Library – Eastern Market – Union Station *See map, pages 18–19*

The first tour explores the geographical center point of the District, Capitol Hill, which, in addition to some of the grandest public buildings, has a good children's museum and a lively market.

Capitol Building

The real crown jewel of the city and perhaps its most characteristic landmark is the ★★★ **United States Capitol ❶** (March to August 9:30am–8pm; September to February 9am–4:30pm; closed Christmas, Thanksgiving and New Year's). Pierre L'Enfant chose one of the most elevated points in his projected city, Jenkins Hill, to be the future home of the most important political site, the U.S. national legislature. An architectural competition was held to find a suitable design for the building, and L'Enfant was to have had the honor of realizing the winning plan, that of architect William Thornton.

But after waiting five months and receiving no designs from the temperamental L'Enfant, Washington lost patience and dismissed him. The task of completing the Capitol finally fell to Benjamin Henry Latrobe, a British architect who had emigrated to the United States in 1796. Latrobe modified Thornton's plan for the south wing to include space for offices and committee rooms. The south wing was completed in 1811, by which time the House had already occupied its new chamber.

In 1814, during the War of 1812, British troops under

Tour bus by Capitol

Admiral Sir George Cockburn burned the Capitol. Although the heavy rain in the evening had put out the fire, the building was left "a most magnificent ruin," as Latrobe lamented. Latrobe was assigned to restore the building, but the costs overran his original estimates and he resigned in 1817. He was succeeded by Charles Bulfinch, who completed the restoration in 1829.

When Congress moved into its new home in 1800, it was only the original south wing that was ready to receive them. The building was smaller than that we see today – it did not yet have its present two outer wings, and it had a smaller, wooden dome covered in copper.

As the country's population grew, so did the number of representatives and senators needed to represent it. So by 1859, two new wings had been added. The new cast-iron dome was inspired by that of St. Isaac's Cathedral in the Russian capital, St. Petersburg. The dome had not been completed when President Lincoln took office in 1861. Many officials wanted to halt construction in order to help pay for the oncoming war. Lincoln ordered that work continue as "a sign we intend the Union shall go on," and the dome was completed in 1863. The 36 columns around the dome represent the 36 states of the Union at the conclusion of the Civil War.

Statue of Freedom

The bronze **Statue of Freedom** that crowns the dome, by sculptor Thomas Crawford, depicts a woman wearing flowing draperies, with her right hand on the sheath of her sword and her left holding a laurel wreath of victory and the shield of the United States with 13 stripes, for the 13 original states.

Between 1874 and 1892, the wooded wilderness that surrounded the Capitol was cleared and the area was expanded and landscaped by Frederick Law Olmsted. He also designed the marble terraces on the north, west, and south top of Capitol Hill that we see today.

Visitors enter the building on the East Front. Be sure to take note of the magnificent bronze ★★ **Columbus Doors** as you enter. Designed by Randolph Rogers, and reminiscent of the great bronze Ghiberti doors of the Baptistry in Florence, Italy, the doors were cast in Munich by the Royal Bavarian Foundry in 1860.

Young visitor admiring the Rotunda

Entering the ★★★ **Rotunda** underneath the Capitol Dome and looking up, you will see the grand canopy by Italian-American artist, Constantino Brumidi, *The Apotheosis of Washington*. This shows Washington surrounded by 13 maidens, and these are, in turn, encircled by figures symbolizing the arts and sciences, the maritime arts, commerce, mechanics, and agriculture.

Just below that, the frieze encircling the Rotunda, depicting events in U.S. history, is also a work begun by Brumidi. In 1879, Brumidi slipped from the scaffold, but

National Statuary Hall

managed to hang on, teetering 58ft (17m) above the floor until help arrived. The incident probably hastened on his death a few months later.

Paintings by John Trumbull adorn the south wall of the Rotunda. Trumbull had served as an aide to General Washington during the Revolutionary War and knew the people whom he was painting. Be sure to visit also the ★★ **Old Senate Chamber**, the Old Supreme Court Room, and the ★ **National Statuary Hall** (the old House chamber). The visitors' galleries of the House of Representatives and Senate can be entered; if the chamber is in session, you must request a pass in advance from the office of your congressman or senator. If you are not a US citizen, bring your passport to the appointments desk of either the House or the Senate, on the first floor, where you will be given a day pass.

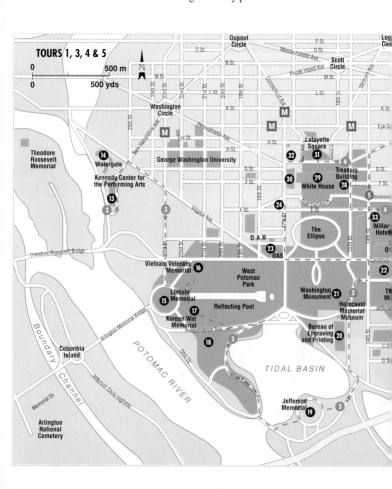

The Capitol has long since grown too small and the business and the staff too large to serve as the offices of senators and congressmen and women. To the north and to the south of the Capitol you will find respectively the **Senate Office** and the **House Office Buildings**. The oldest two of the buildings, the Senate **Russell** and the House **Cannon** Buildings, were both built between 1905 and 1908.

Supreme Court , designed by Cass Gilbert

Moving across from the Capitol, you will arrive at the large Classical façade of the ★ **Supreme Court building** ❷ (Monday to Friday 9am–4:30pm; closed holidays). Constructed in 1934 on the grounds of what had been during the Civil War the Old Capitol Prison, it enabled the Supreme Court, the third branch of government, to move out of the Old Senate Chamber where it had been located since 1860. Visitors may view the Great Hall and the Supreme Court Chamber when the court is not in session.

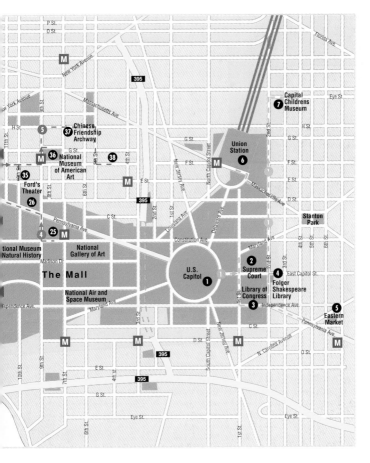

Fountain at Jefferson Building
Great Hall of the Library

Next to the Supreme Court, you'll see the Italian Renaissance-style building which serves as the main building of the **Library of Congress**, the ★★**Thomas Jefferson Building ❸**. The Library of Congress was originally housed in the Capitol itself. When the British burned the Capitol in 1814, they used the contents of the library for kindling. To compensate for this loss to the nation, Thomas Jefferson, then in retirement, sold his own library for less than half its auction value to the government. The Jefferson Building, modeled after the Paris Opéra Garnier, was completed in 1897.

The highlight of the Jefferson Building is the ★★**Great Hall**. You enter the hall on a floor of white marble, into a vast well enclosed in an arcade of two stories. On either side a magnificent staircase leads to the second floor with white marble arches enclosing the arcade space. Above is a heavily-paneled and gold-ornamented ceiling with stained-glass windows.

The library presently contains over 80 million items, filling more than 532 miles (851km) of shelves, and growing at a rate of 7,000 items a day. Over the years it has required two new major additions, the **Adams Building**, situated directly behind the Jefferson Building, and the more modern and spacious **Madison Building**, across the street from the Jefferson on Pennsylvania Avenue.

The Visitors' Center (Monday to Saturday 10am–5:30pm) is located by the ground floor entrance to the Jefferson Building from 1st Street. Guided tours of the building (Monday to Saturday 11:30am, 1pm, 2:30pm, 4pm) allow you to view the magnificent **Main Reading Room** with its 60ft-high (18-m) dome.

From the library, take East Capitol Street one block east to the white marble building on your right. This is the **Folger Shakespeare Library ❹** (Monday to Saturday 10am–4pm, closed holidays). Containing the world's largest collection of the plays and poetry of William Shakespeare, the library serves as a research library for scholars.

Built in 1932 by Henry Clay Folger, the Library was given by Folger to the American people. It is home for the many rare editions of Shakespeare that Folger had collected through the years. By 1930 he had acquired 79 of the approximately 250 surviving copies of the First Folio, the 1623 collected edition of Shakespeare's work. The present collection comprises around 280,000 books and manuscripts, 27,000 paintings, drawings, engravings, and prints, as well as musical instruments, costumes, and films.

A variety of exhibitions are held regularly in the Library's Great Hall. The library also houses an intimate **Elizabethan Theater**, with a three-tiered gallery, which for many years was home to the Shakespeare Theater.

Going south for a few blocks on 7th Street will take you to the **Eastern Market ❺**, one of the few remaining old-style markets that flourished in the city during the 1800s. This stylish, although somewhat barnlike, structure still functions as a market place and is especially vibrant on Saturday mornings, when truck farmers line the stalls outside to sell every variety of homegrown produce.

Go back toward the Capitol on Pennsylvania Avenue and turn right on 2nd Street; this will take you down to ★★ **Union Station ❻**. This magnificent Beaux Arts structure was designed by Daniel Burnham on the model of the monumental baths in ancient Rome. The station opened on October 27, 1907 and was heralded as a showcase terminal of the period. At that time it was the largest train station in the world, designed to handle Inauguration Day crowds of up to 100,000 people. With the decline of the railroads in the 1960s and 1970s, the station became badly neglected, with some voices even calling for the building to be torn down.

    Fortunately, the building was saved. It has been meticulously restored under a public-private partnership, and now houses over 100 upscale shops, nine movie screens and a food court with numerous kiosks offering all sorts of exotic dishes, from Cajun barbecue to sushi. There are also five full-sized restaurants in the building.

    Right behind Union Station, you'll find the **Capital Children's Museum ❼** (September to Easter, daily 10am–5pm; Easter to September, 10am–6pm; closed Thanksgiving, December 25, and New Year's Day). In this hands-on learning center, a child can type on a Braille typewriter, learn Morse code, and print a poster on a Ben Franklin printing press.

Union Station Grand Foyer and Liberty Bell replica

21

Capital Children's Museum

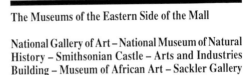

Tour 2

The Museums of the Eastern Side of the Mall

National Gallery of Art – National Museum of Natural History – Smithsonian Castle – Arts and Industries Building – Museum of African Art – Sackler Gallery – Freer Gallery – Hirshhorn Museum – National Air and Space Museum *See map below*

This route along the eastern half of the Mall is a tour of some of the country's finest museums, from the masterpieces of the National Gallery of Art to the astonishing technology displayed in the Air and Space Museum.

The Mall

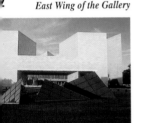

East Wing of the Gallery

Venturing down the Mall from the Capitol toward the Washington Monument, you will first pass on your right a very modern-looking building. This is the East Wing of the ★★★ **National Gallery of Art ❽** (Monday to Saturday, 10am–5pm; Sunday, 11am–6pm; closed January 1, December 25). Completed in 1978 and designed by I.M. Pei (who also designed the pyramid for the Louvre in Paris), the East Wing houses the collection of 20th-century art, as well as many of the Gallery's superb temporary exhibitions. Crossing 4th Street you will come to the Gallery's West Building (the buildings are also connected underground). In designing this neo-Classical structure, architect John Russell Pope (who also designed the National Archives and the Jefferson Memorial) looked for inspiration to the old Court House which once stood nearby. The West Building opened in 1941.

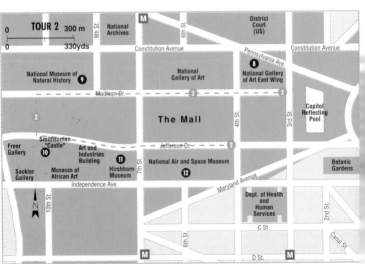

Calder mobile, East Wing

The core of the collection of the National Gallery was Andrew Mellon's donation of 21 masterpieces he purchased from St. Petersburg's Hermitage Museum in 1931, including works by Raphael, Botticelli, and Rembrandt. Mellon (then Secretary of the Treasury) felt that these gifts would be followed by others – and he was right. Other important patrons soon donated works from their collections. Although the Mellon family continues to take an active interest in its development (funds for the East Building were given by Paul Mellon and the late Ailsa Mellon Bruce), the gallery is supported in its daily operations by federal funds. In 1967 the museum acquired the ★ *Portrait of Ginevra da'Benci,* the only painting by Leonardo da Vinci in North America.

Leonardo portrait in the West Wing

The gallery contains paintings and sculpture spanning the last four centuries. Entering the West Wing on the first floor, you will find the collections of American art with paintings by Rembrandt Peale, William Cole, and Gilbert Stuart. Moving up to the second floor you come to European paintings and sculpture, from the 13th through the 19th centuries. One of the high points of your visit will undoubtedly be ★★★ **Room 19**, which contains paintings by Raphael, including his *Cowper Madonna.* The room is dominated by the pristine, serene beauty of the *Alba Madonna.* The bucolic serenity of the scene belies the serious motif of the Infant Christ accepting the cross from the infant John the Baptist. Rembrandt van Rijn is well represented in the Gallery, with one of his self-portraits, *A Polish Nobleman, Lucretia, The Circumcision,* and *The Apostle Paul,* and other paintings and drawings. These are exhibited on the ground floor, near the cafeteria.

Garden Court, West Wing

The Smithsonian "Castle"

Elephant and skeletons in the National Museum of Natural History

After visiting the National Gallery, head further down the Mall. The next building you'll come to is the ★ **National Museum of Natural History** ❾ (daily 10am–5:30pm; closed December 25). The building strongly resembles the West Wing of the National Gallery of Art, and it's easy to get confused. The Museum of Natural History, however, is distinguished by its green dome. This is the nation's largest research museum, with more than 121 million specimens of plants, animals, rocks, gems, minerals, fossils, and human cultural artifacts. Here you can take a trip back in time – to the prehistoric era.

The museum displays a broad spectrum of mineral, plant and animal life as well as artifacts from the early development of man. Already in the rotunda you will find yourself face to face with a life-size African bush elephant – stuffed of course, and much less dangerous than its real-life counterpart. The museum has its own immobile version of Jurassic Park, where you can see, and in one instance, touch the bones of dinosaurs. Look for the skeleton of the Tyrannosaurus Rex, an especially fearsome creature. From the Ice Age, the museum has exhibits displaying a long-tusked American mastodon, a giant ground sloth, a saber-toothed cat and a big-horned bison.

Venturing up to the second floor you can view the world's largest blue diamond, the Hope Diamond, with an interesting history of its own as it traversed the globe passing from kings to commoners. The museum also shows exhibits from early Asian and Pacific cultures and from early Eskimo and Indian cultures.

Heading across the Mall, you will find a building that for the past 150 years has been the symbol of the Smithson ian Institution and, indeed for many years, was the Smithsonian Institution. Affectionately called "**the Castle**"  (daily 9am–5:30pm; closed December 25), the building now serves as the headquarters of the institution as well as the place for visitors to orient themselves in this vast museum complex. The building, with its combination of late Romanesque and early Gothic style, was designed by architect James Renwick, Jr., whose other works included St. Patrick's Cathedral in New York and the Renwick Gallery on Pennsylvania Avenue.

Joseph Henry

The building was the home and laboratory of the first Secretary of the Smithsonian, the scientist Joseph Henry, whose statue stands outside the Castle on the Mall. Henry, whose ground-breaking work in electromagnetism was closely related to similar work by English physicist Michael Faraday and German scientist Karl Gauss, has not achieved the fame his achievements merit. A close friend of Abraham Lincoln, he invented the telegraph, together with Samuel Morse. Henry also helped found the science of meteorology, using weather reports telegraphed in from stations further west; from the tower of the castle, signals would be flashed which could be seen at coastal weather stations. This led to the establishment of the U.S. Weather Service. The building now serves as a general orientation center and administration building for the Smithsonian.

25

Next to the "Castle" stands the Victorian building which was the first home of what was then known as the United States National Museum, now called the ★ **Arts and Industries Building** (daily 10am–5:30pm; closed December 25). The museum opened in 1881, when it served as the site of the inaugural ball of President James A. Garfield. The building originally displayed exhibits acquired from the Centennial Exposition in Philadelphia in 1876. Since that time, the Arts and Industries Building has served as a repository for many of the special exhibits now displayed in the other Smithsonian museums.

Locomotive in the Arts and Industries Building

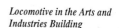

In 1976, the building was restored to its original Victorian style, and a permanent exhibition was set up, "1876," displaying many of the same scientific and techological exhibits that had been first placed on display here in 1881.

By exiting the Arts and Industries Building from the west side, you'll find yourself in the Quadrangle area of the Smithsonian with, as its centerpiece, a beautiful garden, the **Enid A. Haupt Garden**. Changing with the seasons, it features exquisite trees, plants, and flowers.

Directly adjacent to the Arts and Industries Building is the **Museum of African Art** (daily 10am–5:30pm; closed December 25). This is part of a three-level underground museum, research, and education complex that also contains

S. Dillon Ripley Center

Chinese bronzes, Sackler Gallery

the Arthur M. Sackler Gallery and the S. Dillon Ripley Center. The museum collects and exhibits the traditional arts of Africa south of the Sahara, but has also held temporary exhibitions of art from North Africa and Egypt. It is presently adding collections from North Africa. Noteworthy are the museum's sculpture, royal Benin art, and central African ceramics.

Next to the Museum of African Art is the **Arthur M. Sackler Gallery** (daily 10am–5:30pm; closed December 25), containing masterpieces of Asian art. Among the highlights are early Chinese bronzes and jades, Chinese paintings and lacquerware, ancient Near Eastern ceramics and metalware, and sculpture from South and Southeast Asia. The gallery opened in 1987 with a gift of some 1,000 works of Asian art from Dr. Arthur M. Sackler, a research physician and medical publisher from New York City. Supplementing the gallery's holdings are the Vever Collection, an important group of artworks from the Islamic book, spanning the 11th to the 19th centuries, 19th- and 20th-century Japanese prints, and contemporary porcelain. In addition, the Sackler displays numerous temporary exhibitions of Asian art.

Next door to the Sackler is the **Freer Gallery of Art** (daily 10am–5:30pm; closed December 25), which also specializes in art from China, Japan, Korea, South and Southeast Asia and the Near East. The two galleries share a director, and are connected by an underground exhibition space.

The Freer also displays works by the American artist, James McNeill Whistler (1834–1903). Whistler's famous mother is not on exhibit here, but the Peacock Room is. Once the dining room in the London home of Liverpool shipowner Frederick Leyland, the room was decorated with golden peacocks by the American artist, creating an elegant setting for Leyland's blue-and-white porcelain.

Moving back to the Mall, you will pass a small domed structure that appears to be a kiosk. This is the entrance to a very extensive underground complex that houses the offices of Smithsonian Associates, the Smithsonian Office of International Relations as well as the Smithsonian Without Walls program, which examines the future of electronic communication by museums.

Going back down the Mall toward the Capitol, past the Arts and Industries Building, you'll come to a modern circular building that is home to the ★★ **Hirshhorn Museum and Sculpture Garden ⓫** (daily 10am–5:30pm; closed December 25). Before going into the museum, walk down to the Sculpture Garden. Here you will find August Rodin's *Burghers of Calais* as well as a more modernistic *Torso of a Young Man* by the Romanian artist, Constantin Brancusi.

Rodin's Burghers of Calais

Inside the museum, the circular ambulatories on the second floor trace the development of sculpture in Europe from Jean-Baptiste Carpeaux and Edgar Degas through Henri Matisse and Ernst Barlach. On the third floor you will follow the development of modernist art from Picasso and Alberto Giacometti to David Smith and Robert Arnesen. The current trends in modern painting are also exhibited on the third floor.

Continuing down the Mall in the direction of the Capitol, you'll come to the ★★★ **National Air and Space Museum ⑫** (daily 10am–5:30pm; closed December 25). Dedicated on July 4, 1976 during the U.S. Bicentennial celebrations, President Gerald Ford called the museum a gift "from the American people to the American people." Each year, more than 8 million people from all over the world come to the Air and Space Museum to view what is undoubtedly the most impressive collection of air and space artifacts in the world. The museum combines the artifacts with audio-visual exhibits and hands-on experiments that teach the scientific principles behind flight and space travel. In the Samuel P. Langley theater you can view films using the brilliant IMAX projection system with breathtaking scenes of space flight projected onto a screen seven stories wide and five stories high. The film *To Fly* is a perennial favorite.

Immediately on entering the hall from the Mall side, you'll see, hanging from the ceiling, Charles Lindbergh's *Spirit of St. Louis* as well as Chuck Yeager's Bell X-1, the first jet to achieve supersonic flight. Standing upright along the wall are a Pershing II missile and a Russian

Hirshhorn Gallery

27

Aircraft in the National Air and Space Museum

Space exhibits

SS-20 missile. These are the two intermediate-range ballistic missiles that were banned by the 1989 INF Treaty.

Among the aeronautical exhibits are the ★★ **1903 Wright Flyer**, a British Spitfire, a Messerschmidt 109, and the experimental jet version, Messerschmidt Me262. You'll also find here the famed Japanese Zero and a copy of the ★ **P-40 fighter** from the famous Flying Tigers unit which saw service in China during World War II.

In the numerous exhibits on space flight, you'll find a duplicate of the ★★ **Apollo Lunar Module** that carried astronauts to the surface of the Moon in the late 1960s and '70s, a walk-through Skylab mock-up, the first U.S. space station, as well as space suits and rocket engines. Standing in the large Space Hall, you'll also find a replica of the V-2 rocket, the first missile to leave the earth's atmosphere, proving the possibility of space flight. There are also a Jupiter-C and a Vanguard booster rocket which helped launch the first two U.S. satellites in 1958, as well as one of the Saturn F1 engines, five of which propelled the Saturn V rocket that brought the Apollo mission to the moon. The ★★ **Space Race** exhibit, which opened in 1996, shows some of the equipment used by both the U.S. and the Soviet Union in the Cold War-era space race.

A major controversy erupted at the museum when an exhibit on the ★ *Enola Gay*, the B-29 bomber that dropped the atomic bomb over Nagasaki and Hiroshima, opened in 1995. Critics complained that the original exhibit was too negative toward the decision to drop the bomb, claiming that the dropping of the bomb helped speed the Japanese surrender and thus saved many lives. In response to these criticisms, the exhibit was altered to concentrate simply on the display of artifacts from the time. Among these is the fuselage of the bomber and a replic of the "Little Boy" atomic bomb dropped on Hiroshima. The exhibit also gives a history of the unit, the 509th Composite Group which was formed for this mission.

Other exhibits display the development of early flight the ★ **Great War in the Air**, with exhibits from the daredevil days of the dog-fights of World War I; the "golden age" of flight during the inter-war years; and World War II aviation. The exhibit "Where Next, Columbus?" explores the options and possibilities for future space exploration. Nearly all the aircraft and most of the spacecraft in the galleries are genuine. When it is not possible to exhibit a particular spacecraft, the backup vehicle is shown or a replica is made from authentic flight hardware.

Be sure to visit the museum's gift shop which has hundreds of books on space flight, aeronautics, the war in the air, and on general science subjects. Numerous models of the planes and rockets exhibited in the museum can also be found here.

ur 3

Grand Foyer of the Kennedy Center

est Potomac Park, Tidal Basin, and Western Mall

29

**ennedy Center – Lincoln Memorial – Vietnam
terans' Memorial – FDR Memorial – Jefferson
emorial – Bureau of Engraving and Printing –
olocaust Memorial Museum – Washington Monu-
ent – National Museum of American History –
orcoran Gallery of Art** *See map, pages 18–19*

o the west of the Mall are memorials to the country's
eatest presidents, ranging from the arts complex of the
ennedy Center to the towering Washington Monument.
veral important museums are also found on this route.

art the tour from the ★★ **Kennedy Center for the Per-
rming Arts** 🔞 (Monday to Friday 10am–midnight,
unday noon–midnight), just a short walk from the Foggy
ottom Metrorail station, on the Blue and Orange Lines.
egislation for this National Cultural Center was drawn
in 1958, but it was several years before the project
t underway. President Kennedy took the lead in rais-
g funds for the new center, appointing his wife, Jacque-
ne, honorary co-chairwoman of the center.
Boasting a concert hall, an opera house, three theaters
d the American Film Institute, the Kennedy Center can
deed lay claim to the title of the Capital City's cultural
nter. You can enter the Center either through the spa-
ous **Hall of States**, featuring the flags of all 50 states,
e District of Columbia, and the five U.S. territories, or
e equally large **Hall of Nations** with the flags of all na-
ons with which the United States has diplomatic rela-
ons. Both halls lead to the **Grand Foyer**, which provides

Watergate

Lincoln Memorial

Statue of Lincoln by Daniel Chester French

access to the larger theaters – the Concert Hall, Opera House, and Eisenhower Theater. If you were to place the Washington Monument on its side, it would fit inside the Grand Foyer with 75ft (22m) to spare.

The Washington Opera, under the direction of tenor Placido Domingo, is based here. The Center is also the home of the National Symphony Orchestra, now led by Leonard Slatkin, one of the country's most distinguished conductors.

A bust of President Kennedy serves as a centerpiece for the Grand Foyer. Sculptor Robert Berks began working on the bust the night of Kennedy's assassination in 1963.

Going down New Hampshire Avenue, you will see on your left the unmistakable circular buildings of the **Watergate ⓮**. This complex of condominiums and apartments also includes the Watergate Hotel, the site of the burglary of the Democratic National Committee in 1972 that led to the resignation of President Nixon two years later.

Make a right on Virginia Avenue, walking up the hill to 23rd Street. Making another right on 23rd, you will immediately spot the ★★★ **Lincoln Memorial ⓯** (daily 24 hrs, staffed 8am–midnight). Overlooking the grandiose Memorial Bridge, it retains a special place of honor in the city landscape. Built on reclaimed swampland, the front of the memorial looks out over the Reflecting Pool toward the Washington Monument, a fitting extension of the original L'Enfant main axis of the city. The magnificent memorial building is constructed of white Colorado-Yule marble along the classical lines of the great Parthenon in Athens, the temple to the goddess Athena. The outer columns are Doric while the columns inside the hall are Ionic. A magnificent 19-ft (6-m) marble statue by Daniel Chester French of a pensive but resolute Lincoln, seated in a chair, dominates the inner space of the memorial. Below the memorial lies a rectangular pool of water, the Reflecting Pool, which reflects along its 2,000-ft (610-m) length the Washington Monument beyond.

It was only in 1922 that this long-planned memorial was finally dedicated by President Warren G. Harding with Lincoln's only surviving son, Robert Todd Lincoln, in attendance. Inscribed in stone, on an inner wall facing Lincoln's statue, is his Gettysburg Address from 1863, an eloquent plea for the preservation of the republic, spoken at the dedication of a Civil War cemetery in Pennsylvania. Above the address is a frieze showing an Angel of Truth freeing a slave. Lincoln's Second Inaugural Address is inscribed on the opposite wall. The frieze above it depicts the Angel bringing together the two warring sides in reconciliation – the theme of Lincoln's second inaugural.

The monument remains a part of living history. In 1939

e African-American opera singer Marion Anderson had
tempted to hold a concert in Constitution Hall, but was
fused by the Daughters of the American Revolution (who
perated the hall) because of her race. The First Lady,
eanor Roosevelt, was furious; she resigned her DAR
embership and arranged for Miss Anderson to sing from
e steps of the Lincoln Memorial, which she did in front
75,000 people gathered around the Reflecting Pool.
1963, the Reverend Martin Luther King, Jr. gave his up-
ting "I Have a Dream" speech at that same spot.

short walk down from the Lincoln Memorial to the left
the Reflecting Pool will take you to the ★★ **Vietnam
eterans' Memorial** ❶. When the memorial was
anned, many people thought that the two polished, black
anite walls, V-shaped and half-buried, bearing the names
the 58,000 American soldiers who died in the Viet-
m War, was too negative a memorial of what had been
very controversial war. In response to this criticism, an
ditional heroic sculpture by Frederick Hart of three Viet-
m-era soldiers was erected just opposite, with the three
ldiers facing the wall.

*Vietnam War soldiers,
by Frederick Hart*

31

"The Wall," as it is commonly known, has proved to be
e of Washington's most popular memorials – as well
a most personal one. The names are inscribed on the
emorial in the chronological order in which the sol-
ers died. At the two entrances to the ramp leading down
the center of the memorial, visitors can refer to books
which the names of the deceased are recorded in al-
abetical order, and can find out exactly where each
ldier is named on the memorial wall.

*Vietnam Veterans'
Memorial*

Korean War Veterans' Memorial

Veterans' memorabilia

Close by "The Wall" is a third Vietnam memorial, the **Vietnam Women's Memorial**, dedicated to the 265,000 women who served during the 12 years of the Vietnam War in the Army, Navy, Air Force, Marines or other government agencies or as volunteers in humanitarian organizations such as the USO or Red Cross. Ninety percent of the women served as nurses. The Memorial was dedicated in November 1993.

Another, more recent addition to the memorials surrounding the Reflecting Pool is the **Korean War Veterans' Memorial** ⓱. A short walk to the other side of the pool will take you to this almost life-like group of soldiers sculpted in stainless steel, marching in loose combat formation as if they were on patrol. As you walk alongside the group toward the apex of the triangle formed by the figures, you experience the eerie feeling of marching along with them. As you travel from the apex back down to the base of the triangular formation you walk beside a black granite wall. Hundreds of images of soldiers from the Korean War have been carefully sandblasted into the stone.

Further down Independence Avenue toward the Washington Monument, you will pass on your right the **Franklin Delano Roosevelt Memorial** ⓲, dedicated in May, 1997. Look carefully, as the entrance to the memorial can't be seen from the road.

President Roosevelt crafted the New Deal which helped pull the country out of the 1930s Depression and then led the nation through World War II – a memorial to him was long overdue. There was already a monument to Roosevelt in Washington – one which was wholly in accord with his own wishes. When asked what form his commemoration should take, Roosevelt had replied that he wanted a stone slab "no bigger than my desk" placed in front of the National Archives on Pennsylvania Avenue. Until 1997, this slab had been Roosevelt's only memorial in the Capital City.

The new memorial, covering a full 7.5 acres (3 hectares) along the Cherry Tree Walk at the Tidal Basin, is one of the country's most expansive. The soft red South Dakota granite walls constitute four open-air rooms, each signifying one of Roosevelt's four terms of office. More than 6,000 tons of granite were required. The walls of the various rooms are interspersed with shade trees, quiet alcoves and waterfalls – symbolic of Roosevelt's love of water as well as his massive Tennessee Valley Authority project which brought hydroelectric power to millions.

On the walls are quotes from Roosevelt, summing his philosophy and policies. There is a 9-ft (2.7-m) bronze statue of a seated Roosevelt in his Navy cape, with

Jefferson Memorial

ver-present Scotch terrier, Fala, by his side. In the last
room is a bronze statue of his wife Eleanor Roosevelt,
whom President Truman later appointed the first U.S. Ambassador to the United Nations.

Just opposite the FDR Memorial, on the other side of the
Tidal Basin, is the ★★ **Jefferson Memorial** ⑲ (daily
8am–11:45pm). This memorial to the third president, and
chief author of the Declaration of Independence, was dedicated by Franklin D. Roosevelt in 1943. The design of the
memorial building is inspired by Rome's Pantheon, an architectural model used by the amateur architect Jefferson himself, for example in the design of his home in
Monticello (*see page 74*) and for the University of Virginia in Charlottesville. In the center of the memorial,
which is open to the elements, stands a 19-ft (5.8-m)
bronze statue of Jefferson on a 6-ft (1.8-m) high pedestal
of Minnesota granite. Jefferson is wearing the fur coat that
was given him by his friend, Taddeus Kosciusko, the Polish patriot and veteran of the Revolutionary War.

*Relaxing at the
Tidal Basin*

Jefferson looks out over the Tidal Basin, which in early
April is surrounded by the soft pink and white blossoms
of the Japanese cherry trees given by Japan to the city of
Washington in 1912. Another 3,800 trees were donated by
Japan in 1965 and accepted by the First Lady, Lady Bird
Johnson. The trees blossom for two weeks in late March
and early April; they are at their peak for a mere three days.
The annual Cherry Blossom Festival attracts huge crowds
from across the nation.

Continue along the Tidal Basin and up Raoul Wallenberg
Place (15th Street). You will come to the **Bureau of En-**

*Bureau of Engraving
and Printing*

graving and Printing **⑳** (tours every 10 minutes, Ap
to September, 9am–1:50pm; evening tours, June to A
gust, every 10 minutes; tickets required April to Septe
ber; October to March, tours 9am–2pm, no ticke
required). The tour takes you through the process of pri
ing money, and in the Visitors Center you can buy shre
ded bills or even a ream of uncut bills.

Holocaust Museum

Just next door to the Bureau of Engraving and Prir
ing is the ★ **Holocaust Memorial Museum** (daily 10ar
5:30pm). Chartered by a unanimous Act of Congress
1980, the Holocaust Museum was set up to "advance a
disseminate knowledge" about the Nazi Holocau.
Opened in 1993, the museum's Permanent Exhibition tel
the story of the Jews targeted for annihilation by the Na
in the 1930s and during World War II. It also describes t
fate of other victims of that genocide – gypsies, Pole
homosexuals, the handicapped, and political and religio
dissidents. Using artifacts, oral histories, documenta
film, and photographs, the museum gives a graphic d
scription of the Holocaust, with remarkable film foota
from the Nazi era.

34

The museum also contains a Hall of Remembrance.
six-sided, 60-ft (19-m) high, 6,000 sq ft (555 sq m) stru
ture illuminated by a skylight. This is a national memc
ial to the victims of the Holocaust.

The Permanent Exhibition requires a timed entry pas
Passes are free and are not required for the museum's oth
exhibitions, memorial, resources, and facilities.

*Reflecting Pool and
Washington Monument*

Cross over to the ★★ **Washington Monument** **㉑** (Ap
to September, daily 8am–11:45pm; October to Marc
9am–4:45pm). The 555-ft (170-m) giant stone obelisk, de
icated to George Washington, can be seen for miles aroun
Its location was chosen by L'Enfant in his original pla
of the city, but he had envisioned an equestrian statue.

The cornerstone of the monument was laid in July 184
but lack of money and the onset of the Civil War in 186
delayed its completion for many years. In 1877, work c
the monument resumed, and it was completed in 188
The difference in coloration of the stone in the mon
ment between the lower third of the statue and the upp
two-thirds is a result of that extended delay.

Inside the monument are memorial stones which wer
donated as gifts of the 50 states, as well as numerous g
stones from foreign governments, organizations, citie
and individuals. An elevator will take you in 70 secon
to the top of the monument where you can get a breat
taking panoramic view of the city. Free tickets for a time
entrance are available at the ticket kiosk on 15th Stre
at the base of the monument. During the height of th
tourist season, however, ticket lines can be long.

The $500,000 grant by British scientist and philanthropist James Smithson to set up the Smithsonian Institution as "an establishment for the increase and diffusion of knowledge" was aimed primarily at the promotion of science and technology in the new republic. The field of knowledge that was originally envisioned has, however, expanded with the years – and with increased funding. The ★★ **National Museum of American History** ㉒ (daily 10am–5:30pm; closed December 25) records much of the development of technology in the United States since the country's founding.

National Museum of American History

One exhibit that you won't fail to notice as you enter the museum from the Mall entrance (which is on the second floor) is the great Foucault Pendulum hanging from the ceiling. A 240lb (110kg) brass bob swings back and forth, knocking down one by one the red markers arranged in a circle on the floor. This clearly demonstrates the axial rotation of the earth, as the circle on the ground must be turning, since the plane in which the pendulum swings does not change.

On the ground floor, railroad buffs can view a Pacific-type steam locomotive built for the Southern Railroad in 1926. At regular intervals, the locomotive is started up and the whistle blown as if the locomotive were ready to roll. Tunnel-digging equipment is also on display as well as a detailed exhibit on bridge-building, with examples of the various types of bridge design. A large exhibit on the "Information Age" goes through the history of information technology, taking the viewer from the Morse telegraph and Alexander Graham Bell's telephone to the computer era, showing the development from ENIAC computers all the way to modern microcomputers.

Foucault Pendulum

Typesetting machines

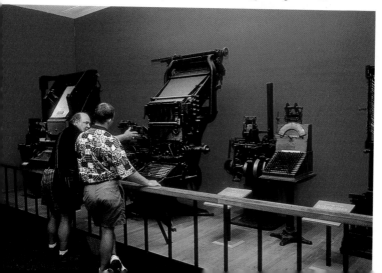

There is also an exhibit on the development of heavy power machinery, illustrating the harnessing of atmospheric force, the early age of steam power and the development of high-pressure and high-speed engines. Eli Whitney's cotton gin as well as the desk on which Thomas Jefferson wrote the Declaration of Independence are on display here. Other exhibits show the development of music in America. Always a very popular exhibit is the museum's display of the gowns of the First Ladies, from Mrs. Taft to Hillary Clinton. Also on display is the original flag that flew over Fort Henry in Baltimore, inspiring poet Francis Scott Key to write the words to the national anthem, "The Star Spangled Banner," during the British attack in 1814. There is also a Hands-On Science Center, that allows visitors to learn scientific principles in a genuine spirit of play and invention. The bookstore in the basement of the museum is well worth the browsing time.

Antique violins in the National Museum of American History

Head west back down Constitution Avenue and turn right on 17th Street. Right across from you is the headquarters of the **Organization of American States ㉓** (Monday to Friday 9am–5:30pm). Originally called the Pan-American Union, the organization encompasses 35 member nations from North, South, and Central America, and the Caribbean. The Beaux Arts hacienda was built in 1910 with money donated by Andrew Carnegie. A statue of Queen Isabella of Spain, who financed Columbus's voyage to the New World, adorns the entrance. On the ground floor a small gallery exhibits art from member nations.

Continue north on 17th Street for one block and you'll come to **Constitution Hall** and **Continental Hall**, where the Museum of the Daughters of the American Revolution (Monday to Friday 8:30am–4pm; Sunday 1–5pm) is located. The museum features an outstanding collection of decorative and fine arts made or used in America between 1700 and 1850. The 33 State Period Rooms and two galleries each represent a particular historic period or region, including a 17th-century New England one-room house, an 18th-century tavern, and a 19th-century kitchen.

THE CORCORAN GALLERY OF ART

Outside the Corcoran Gallery of Art

Walk two blocks further on 17th Street and you'll arrive at the ★ **Corcoran Gallery of Art ㉔**. Housed in a beautiful Beaux Arts building across from the Old Executive Office Building, the Corcoran contains an excellent collection of paintings and sculpture, including works by Monet, Degas, and Renoir. The high point of the museum is the American collection. A portrait of George Washington by Gilbert Stuart, a few paintings by Albert Bierstadt, portraits of Civil War Generals Grant and Lee, a painting by the inventor Samuel F.B. Morse, *The Old House of Representatives*, are well worth a look.

Tour 4

Pennsylvania Avenue

National Archives – J. Edgar Hoover Building (FBI) – Old Post Office Pavilion – White House – Lafayette Square – Renwick Gallery *See map, pages 18–19*

This tour takes you up Pennsylvania Avenue, away from the Congressional branch of government and toward the Executive, in the form of the White House and its administrative buildings. Along the way are two important sights, the National Archives and FBI headquarters, plus the Old Post Office, now converted into a food hall and shopping mall.

Pennsylvania Avenue

We start our tour at the stately ★ **National Archives Building 25** (September to March, daily 10am–5:30pm; April to August, 10am–9pm). The entire history of the United States is chronicled here. In this building, built in Greek Revival style by John Russell Pope, are stored some of the earliest documents relating to the United States, including original examples of the Declaration of Independence of 1776, the U.S. Constitution, and the Bill of Rights, which are on permanent display. Expect to wait in line when going to see them, however.

National Archives

Moving around to Pennsylvania Avenue, you will come to the ★ **J. Edgar Hoover Building 26**, since 1975 the home of the Federal Bureau of Investigation (tours Monday to Friday, 8:45am–4:15pm). Hoover was the head of the FBI from 1924 until he died in 1977 at the age of 77, and led campaigns against gangsters and Communists. The tour is fun for kids over kindergarten age who will enjoy the display of gangster paraphernalia and relics of some of the "bad guys" from the Prohibition era of the 1920s. The highpoint is a marksmanship demonstration by an Agent using a Smith and Wesson or a Thompson submachine gun. Lines can be long during the tourist season.

Looking up Pennsylvania Avenue toward 12th Street, you'll see one of the most unusual buildings in Washington. This Romanesque structure with a very tall tower served for many years as the Old Post Office (summer, daily 8am–10:45pm; winter, 10:00am–5:45pm), now known as the ★ **Pavilion 27**. At the time of its construction in 1899, it was the largest government building in Washington (over 12 stories high) and the first to have a clock tower. Today it is an indoor mall, a prime attraction for tourist groups looking for an inexpensive place to eat. Many fast-food chains have booths here with tables placed in the large open area which is open all the way

Food Hall at the Pavilion, and view from the Tower

to the ceiling 12 stories up, where a skylight provides illumination. Tours for the Old Post Office Tower give visitors a bird's eye view from the Observation Deck 270ft (82m) above Pennsylvania Avenue.

Continuing down Pennsylvania Avenue to 15th Street, you will come upon the imposing ★ **Treasury Building** ㉘. Construction was begun in 1833 by Robert Mills, the architect of the Washington Monument. Due to restrictions on funding by Congress, Mill had to used sandstone from government quarries instead of the granite he preferred for the exterior. From 1855 to 1869, two wings were added, this time in granite, creating an impressive structure in Greek Revival style. The building was the first major departure from the L'Enfant plan, interrupting the grand vista of Pennsylvania Avenue from the White House to the Capitol. Legend has it that President Andrew Jackson, wishing to end the eternal dispute over the building's location, came out of the White House, pointed his cane to the spot, and said "Build it here!"

After some years of neglect, the building was restored to its original splendor in 1985. Serving as the office of the Treasury Department, the building is also available for tours – but only if you call at least a week in advance. Tel. (202) 622-0692.

South portico of the White House

Next to the Treasury Building is the ★★★ **White House** ㉙, the home of the President and his family (self-guided tours Tuesday–Saturday 10am–noon; timed tickets distributed from the White House Visitor Center at 15th Street near E Street). After an architectural competition, a design for the house by an Irish architect, James Hoban, was chosen. (Thomas Jefferson had also submitted a design to the competition – but anonymously.) Hoban's design drew on the Palladian architecture of mid-18th century Europe and there are striking similarities between the White House and the Irish Parliament in Dublin, Leinster House.

Construction on the house began in 1792, but proceeded so slowly that it was not completed during George Washington's presidency. On November 1, 1800, President John Adams took up residence in the still unfinished mansion and the capital of the United States was thus officially transferred from Philadelphia to Washington. Until the presidency of Theodore Roosevelt (1901–8), the building was known officially as the Executive Mansion.

On August 24, 1814, the White House and adjoining government buildings were set on fire by British Army units under Admiral George Cockburn. Heavy rains that night put out the fires and saved the building from total devastation. Marks from the fire can still be seen on the White House. The original furnishings were destroyed in the fire, and much of the older furniture that remains today dates back, therefore, to after 1817, when President James Monroe moved in to the restored building.

North portico of the White House

The renovation of the gutted building led to further alterations. In 1824 Hoban added the semicircular south portico after a design created by Benjamin Latrobe for Thomas Jefferson. Five years later the impressive north portico was added under the skilled supervision of Latrobe himself. Gas lighting was installed in 1848, city water in 1853, bathrooms around 1878, and electricity in 1890. Air-conditioning didn't arrive until 1909.

At one time, Americans could enter the White House at noon to meet the president, who would allocate an hour in his daily schedule to shake their hands. By 1928, when Herbert Hoover was president, the number of daily visitors had increased to more than 1,000, and the practice had to be discontinued.

Tourists straining for a view of the President

In 1995 a man stood in front of the White House and began shooting at the house; fortunately, he was overpowered by bystanders before any real harm was done. The incident resulted, however, in heightened security precautions and the closing of Pennsylvania Avenue to traffic between 16th Street and 17th Street. The area is now an excellent walking street, and is often used for roller skating and roller hockey games.

The increasing need for workspace in the White House has not led to changes in its fundamental contours – despite extravagant proposals over the years. In 1902, Theodore Roosevelt added a graceful covered colonnade extending from the West Wing of the house, at the end of which is a one-story structure that serves as the president's offices: the Oval Office. This is visible only from the Pennsylvania Avenue side of the White House.

Photo opportunity

Even with timed tickets there may be a long wait to start your White House tour. Entering from the East Portico, you'll pass the White House Library on your right. The president, his family and staff still draw on its resources. You will also pass the Vermeil Room, once a billiard room but now exhibiting some of the White House silver gilt.

Going up the steps you'll enter the fabulous East Room. Best known as the site of presidential press conferences, the East Room was planned by Hoban as a public reception room. It has been the site for the numerous balls and galas that take place regularly at the White House. The coffins of seven presidents have lain in state in the East Room, including Lincoln, McKinley, and Kennedy.

Along the tour you will see portraits of many of the presidents. On the wall of the East Room hangs a very famous portrait of George Washington by Gilbert Stuart, the only object in the White House that has been there since the Adamses moved in – only a few items were rescued by staff when the British attacked in 1814. During the Civil War, Union soldiers were quartered briefly in the East Room. In 1886, President Grover Cleveland was married in this room. On the wall of the East Room is a fine painting of President William McKinley.

Your tour will continue through the Green Room, which served as Jefferson's dining room; the Oval Blue Room, with the ornate French furniture brought to the White House by President Monroe after the 1814 fire; the Red Room; and the State Dining Room, which seats around 150 people. You'll then go out to the grand Cross Hall and exit the building through the North Entrance Portico.

The colonnade building leading to the Oval Office is

The South Lawn

where President Franklin D. Roosevelt, who suffered from polio, built an indoor swimming pool for his needed exercise. During the Nixon Administration the pool was covered over and the space made into the White House Press Briefing Room.

Earlier, in 1927, President Calvin Coolidge had expanded the attic into a third floor. This put a great deal of weight on the wooden beams of the second floor. By the time Truman arrived in 1947, it was discovered that the heavy frescoed ceiling of the East Room was beginning to sag. Truman wisely decided to move with his family to Blair House across the street while the White House was gutted and rebuilt with a strengthened frame.

While at Blair House, an unsuccessful attempt was made on Truman's life by Puerto Rican fanatics. A Secret Service officer charged with protecting the President was, however, killed in the attempt. It was also during the Truman reconstruction of the White House that the Truman Balcony was added to the south portico.

The balcony can be viewed from the south side of the building on E Street. Here you can also see President's Park where the Rose Garden is located, the site of many outdoor press conferences. It is also here that the President receives foreign dignitaries in formal military ceremonies, often with the famous Fifes and Drum Corps, whose origins date back to the American Revolution.

Old Executive Office Building, built in 1888

Next to the White House is the **Old Executive Office Building** ㉚ (OEOB) (free tours Saturday 9–11:30am). Here are the offices of the Vice President and the National Security Council, and many of the numerous offices connected to the Executive Branch. Despite the downsizing of government, the building is no longer sufficient for the business of the president and a New Executive Office Building has been built further up on 17th Street.

The massive granite structure of the OEOB, designed by architect Alfred B. Mullet in the then popular French Second Empire style, was completed in 1888, consolidating into one large building the three buildings that previously housed the State, War, and Navy offices. At that time, the building was the largest office building in the world. More than 1,000 treaties have been signed here.

Lafayette statue in Lafayette Square

We can thank Thomas Jefferson for the leafy expanse of **Lafayette Square** ㉛, just across from the White House. This was originally attached to the presidential residence, but Jefferson, ever mindful that the new republic should be ruled by a humble president and not a grandiose king, decided that the 7-acre (3-hectare) plot was too large. He decreed that the green space should be cut in two by Pennsylvania Avenue, with the new park, called President's

Statue of Andrew Jackson

St. John's Episcopal Church and Parish House

Square, to the north. In 1824, an enormous public reception was held here for the Marquis de Lafayette, the French general who had assembled an army and crossed the Atlantic to help the colonists win independence from the British, and the park was renamed in his honor. Lafayette's statue stands in the southeast corner.

In the center of the park is an equestrian statue of Andrew Jackson, erected in 1853 to commemorate his victory over the British at the Battle of New Orleans in 1815. British cannonballs were smelt to provide the iron. In the northeast corner of the park is a statue of Thaddeus Kosciuszko. During the American Revolution, he built the fortifications at West Point and Saratoga before returning to his native Poland to fight its war of independence against Russia.

In the southwest corner stands a statue of Count de Rochambeau, who led the French Expeditionary Force sent to assist General Washington. Finally in the northwest corner stands the statue of Baron von Steuben, the Prussian officer who trained Washington's men at Valley Forge during the harsh winter of 1777–8.

Just on the other side of Lafayette Park, you will find the small Greek Revival church, ★ **St. John's Episcopal Church**, which was designed by Benjamin Latrobe in 1816. The stained-glassed windows of the church were designed by Veuve Lorin, curator of stained-glass windows at Chartres Cathedral. Since the early 1800s, every president has come to worship at this "Church of the Presidents." (Pew 54 in the church is the president's pew.) The steeple bell, given by President Monroe, was cast from a British cannon.

The Parish House next door was once the home of Alexander Baring, Lord Ashburton, the British minister who negotiated the U.S.–Canadian boundary treaty in 1842. Ashburton's negotiating partner, Daniel Webster, lived right down the street. Since they were both gourmands they would invite each other to dinner, each trying to outdo the other as host. This seems to have taken the edge off what were otherwise rancorous negotiations. After Ashburton's tenure, the house served as the British legation until 1852.

Crossing over to the park side of H Street and continuing west toward 17th Street, you arrive at **Decatur House**, purchased in 1819 by Commodore Stephen Decatur, a naval hero in the battles against the Barbary pirates and in the War of 1812. In 1819, Decatur used the prize money he had won in his victories to build the first private house on President's Square. He didn't have much time to enjoy his new home, however, as he was killed in a duel the following year.

Renwick Gallery

43

The building was designed by Benjamin Henry Latrobe. A prime example of the Federal style, the house has changed hands numerous times, serving as the residence of such notable political figures as Henry Clay, Martin Van Buren, and Judah Benjamin. For a short time the building was leased to the Russian Minister and functioned as the Russian legation. The building was bequeathed to the National Trust for Historic Preservation and for many years has been the national headquarters of the Trust. Two floors of the building, furnished in Federal style, are open to the public (Tuesday to Friday 10am–3pm, Saturday and Sunday noon–4pm).

Head down to 17th Street and back to Pennsylvania Avenue. On the corner is the **Renwick Gallery** ㉜ (daily 10am–5:30pm, closed December 25), which in 1859 was the first building in French Second Empire style in the United States. The Renwick is part of the National Museum of American Art and displays a permanent exhibit of some 450 objects of glass, metal, ceramics, wood, and fiber by American artists. In addition the Renwick stages exhibitions on major issues in American crafts and decorative arts.

During the Civil War, the building was used as a headquarters and a warehouse by Union Quartermaster General Montgomery Meigs. From 1874 until 1897, the building housed the art collection of William Wilson Corcoran and was the first art museum in the city. When the Corcoran moved to its new location just two blocks down 17th Street *(see page 36)*, the Renwick served as the location of the U.S. Court of Claims. In 1965, the building was transferred to the Smithsonian Institution and renamed for its architect, James Renwick.

Sidewalk flower stall

Tour 5

Downtown Washington

Willard Hotel – National Museum of Women in the Arts – Ford's Theater – National Portrait Gallery – National Museum of American Art – Chinatown – National Building Museum *See map, pages 18–19*

VIP at the Willard Hotel

Scattered among Washington's downtown office and shopping area you will find some important historic sights, plus several museums which are well worth a visit.

The ★ **Willard Hotel ❸**, at 14th and Pennsylvania Avenue, N.W., has always played an important role in the history of the city. What you see today, however, is the New Willard Hotel, built in 1901. The "old" Willard dated back to 1801, when it was known as the City Hotel.

Abraham Lincoln stayed at the Willard for 10 days in 1861 when he came to Washington with his family to be inaugurated as president. His bill for $773.75 is in the small room off the grand corridor with other memorabilia. Other guests have included Edward VII (when Prince of Wales), Jenny Lind, Charles Dickens, and Buffalo Bill Cody. Julia Ward Howe was staying at the Willard when she composed the text to the "Battle Hymn of the Republic," which became the unofficial anthem of the Union cause in the Civil War. The story goes that she was awakened by Union soldiers marching past, and wrote the words on hotel stationery. Later, Mark Twain wrote two of his books here. After a long period of decline, this grand old hotel was renovated in 1986.

Go north on 14th Street from the Willard and make a right on New York Avenue down to 13th Street. Here you'll find the **National Museum of Women in the Arts ❸** (Monday to Saturday, 10am–5pm; Sunday, noon–5pm), opened in 1987. The museum's permanent collection contains paintings, drawings, sculpture, pottery, prints, books, and photography by women from the Renaissance to the modern era, including works by such prominent artists as Georgia O'Keefe and Helen Frankenthaler.

Box where Lincoln was shot, at Ford's Theater

Walk south on 12th Street to F Street and turn left. Make another right on 10th Street and walk a half block down the street. Here you'll find ★★ **Ford's Theater ❸**, where President Lincoln was shot by a deranged actor and Confederate sympathizer, John Wilkes Booth, on April 14, 1865 (daily 9am–5pm; closed during matinees and rehearsals, and December 25).

The box where Lincoln was shot is maintained as it was

hen as a memorial. Ford's is again operating as a func-
ioning theater, and the president still comes to view its
roductions, although now his seat is in the front row. The
Lincoln Museum in the basement is well worth a visit,
ven if, due to rehearsals or matinee performances, the
heater is inaccesible.

Across the street you can visit the **Petersen House**
daily 9am–5pm; closed December 25), where the
wounded Lincoln was taken. Three rooms, including the
ne where Lincoln died the morning after the shooting,
re decorated in Victorian style.

Petersen House

Go back up to G Street and turn right. A short trek will
ake you past the Martin Luther King Library to a large
Greek Revival building, the Old Patent Office. Today it
s the home of both the ★ **National Portrait Gallery** and
he **National Museum of American Art 36** (both gal-
eries open daily 10am–5:30pm; closed December 25).

Construction on the building began in 1836. In March,
865 it was the site of Lincoln's second inaugural ball.
During the Civil War it functioned as a hospital with 2,000
eds on the marble floors to cope with the wounded. The
oet Walt Whitman worked here as a volunteer nurse.

45

The National Portrait Gallery, which is entered from
F Street, contains portraits, drawings, and photographs
f individuals who, in the words of the Congressional di-
ective establishing it, "have made significant contribu-
ions to the history, development, and culture of the people
f the United States." Look out for the Gilbert Stuart por-
raits of George Washington and Thomas Jefferson, pho-
ographs of Abraham Lincoln by Mathew Brady, the Edgar
Degas portrait of Mary Cassatt, and the portraits of Amer-
can performers, such as actress Tallulah Bankhead painted

National Portrait Gallery

Chinese Friendship Archway

by Augustus John. On the top floor you will find the Museum of Models, with some memorabilia from the time when the building served as the U.S. Patent Office.

A walk around to the G Street entrance of the building will take you into the National Museum of American Art. This is the oldest national art collection in the country, with paintings from such notable American artists as Albert Bierstadt, Winslow Homer, Charles Willson Peale, and George Catlin.

Walk north up to H Street, turn right and walk one block further, where you will pass at 7th and H Streets the Chinese Friendship Archway marking the entrance to **Chinatown ③**. This decorative entrance was built by the District government in coordination with the Municipality of Beijing. Chiefly a commercial area, here you will find many shops, and very good restaurants.

Continuing past Chinatown on H Street, make a right on 5th Street down to F Street. Here is located the enormous, red brick, Renaissance-style building which houses the **National Building Museum ③** (Monday to Saturday 10am–4pm; Sunday noon–4pm).

Built in 1881–7 to provide offices for the 1,500 clerks of the U.S. Pension Bureau, the building utilized all the latest in sky-lighting, ventilation, and fireproofing, and required some 15.5 million bricks. The extremely impressive open space inside, known as the Great Hall, measures 316ft (96m) by 116ft (35m), with a roof reaching 159ft (48m). Visitors can see artifacts and records from the field of the building arts, including drawings, photographs, and documents.

National Building Museum

Tour 6

Georgetown

Old Stone House – C&O Canal – Georgetown University – Dumbarton Oaks – Tudor Place – Cox's Row
See map, pages 48–9

No visitor should leave Washington without enjoying a stroll through the narrow, leafy streets of its oldest area, Georgetown. Several of the historic houses are open to the public, and there is good shopping along M Street and Wisconsin Avenue.

Elegant Georgetown house

Georgetown was a thriving commercial town long before Washington, D.C. had even been conceived. Established as a tobacco port, it received its charter in 1751. Large sailing ships were easily able to navigate the Potomac from the Chesapeake Bay all the way to Georgetown's ports. Georgetown had mills, factories, and a customs house. Its fleet of cargo ships sailed to Europe and the West Indies laden with tobacco and returned with furniture and luxury goods.

Harbor development in Georgetown

Even after the establishment of Washington, Georgetown continued to flourish. By the 1820s, however, the river had begun to silt up, making river traffic more difficult and therefore harming Georgetown's economy.

A prime example of the older Georgetown is the **Old Stone House** ❸❾ (daily 9am–5pm; closed government holidays) which stands, with its small colonial garden, somewhat alone among the finery of Georgetown's M Street, one of the main commercial arteries. Built in 1765 by Christopher Lehman, the house was used both as a home and a workshop. Lehman was a cabinetmaker by trade and had his shop on the ground floor.

Part of Georgetown's prosperity came from the **Chesapeake & Ohio (C&O) Canal** ❹⓿, which had its terminus there. In 1828 the states of Maryland, Virginia, and Pennsylvania chartered the Company to build a canal with 74 locks from Georgetown to Cumberland, Maryland – a stretch of 184 miles (294km). On July 4th of that year, President John Quincy Adams turned the first shovel of earth on the canal construction. Ironically, on that same day Charles Carroll of Maryland, one of the signers of the Declaration of Independence, was turning the first shovel of dirt on the Baltimore and Ohio (B&O) Railroad, which was planned to take a similar route to the Ohio Valley.

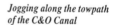

Jogging along the towpath of the C&O Canal

The construction and successful completion of the canal gave new life to the Georgetown economy, although the development of the B&O Railroad would quickly over-

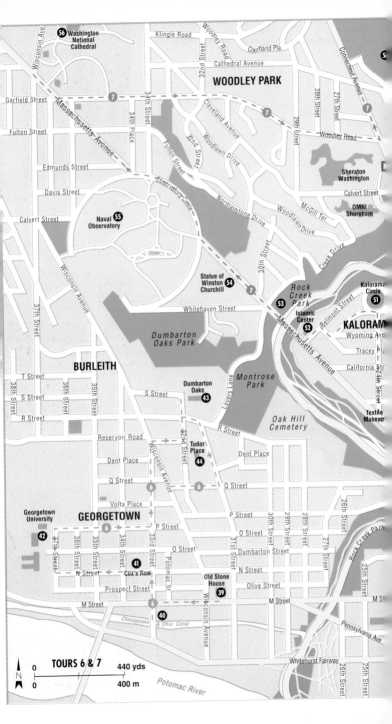

56 Washington National Cathedral

Klingle Road

Courtland Pla

Cathedral Avenue

WOODLEY PARK

Garfield Street

7

Cleveland Avenue

7

Woodley Road

Fulton Street

Edmunds Street

Observatory Circle

Normanstone Drive

Sheraton Washington

Calvert Street

Davis Street

Woodlawn Drive

McGill Ter

OMNI Shoreham

Calvert Street

55 Naval Observatory

Creek Drive

Kalorama Circle **51**

Statue of Winston Churchill **54**

7

53

Rock Creek Park

KALORAM

Whitehaven Street

Islamic Center **52**

Wyoming Ave

Belmont Street

Tracey Pla

BURLEITH

Dumbarton Oaks Park

Montrose Park

California Str

T Street

Dumbarton Oaks **43**

Lovers Lane

Oak Hill Cemetery

Textile Museo

S Street

S Street

R Street

Reservoir Road

R Street

Dent Place

Dent Place

Tudor Place **44**

Q Street

Q Street

Volta Place

GEORGETOWN

Georgetown University

42

P Street

P Street

O Street

Dumbarton Street

O Street

41 Cox's Row

N Street

N Street

Old Stone House **39**

Prospect Street

Olive Street

M Street

M Street

Chesapeake

40

& Ohio Canal

Pennsylvania Ave

Whitehurst Fairway

TOURS 6 & 7

0 — 440 yds

0 — 400 m

Potomac River

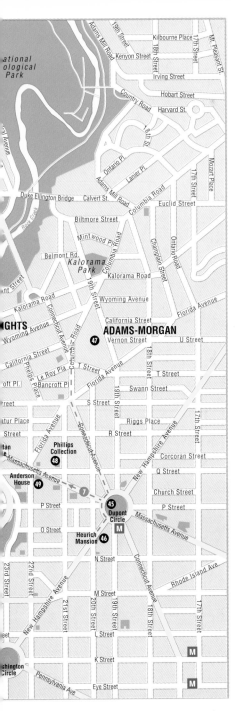

*West Front of the
National Cathedral*

49

*Georgetown University's
Healy Hall*

Lions at the Zoo

shadow the canal's importance as a means of transporting goods. In 1889 a huge flood destroyed much of the canal, and its bridges, banks and locks. The canal went into receivership to the B&O Railroad, which operated it until another severe flood hit in 1924, which caused it to be closed for good.

The canal is today run by the National Park Service. Severe floods in 1996 also left the canal in shambles, but it has been rebuilt for most of the way. You can walk along the canal in Georgetown, and, except for extremely dry periods, there's water in it. From Georgetown you can also take a trip on a canal boat, pulled, as was done in the old days, by horse or mule (Visitors' Center, April to October, daily 10am–4pm; boat tours Wednesday to Sunday 11am, 1pm, and 3 pm).

Cox's Row

Every street of Georgetown is filled with history. Iron plaques on many of the houses provide information on their past. Of special note is the area known as ★ **Cox's Row** ④, on the north side of the block of 3300 N Street. This row of houses was built in 1817 by Colonel John Cox, the mayor of Georgetown. It was at 3337 N Street that the Marquis de Lafayette *(see page 41)* stayed during his celebrated return visit to the United States in 1824. Cox's former home at 3339 N Street later became the home of Commodore Charles Morris, a naval hero of the war against the Barbary pirates in 1801. Of more recent fame is the house at No. 3307 which was purchased by Senator John F. Kennedy for his wife Jacqueline after the birth of their first child, Caroline.

Georgetown University's Healy Hall

One of Georgetown's more important sites is **Georgetown University** ④, located on a steep hill overlooking

the Potomac. The university was founded in 1789 by Bishop John Carroll of Maryland, a cousin of one of the signers of the Declaration of Independence. Although it was the first Roman Catholic university in the country, Carroll specified that it should educate "students of every religious profession." Two of George Washington's nephews were enrolled at Georgetown. In 1829 President Andrew Jackson sent his grandnephew to Georgetown "to get some discipline." Georgetown's astronomical observatory, founded in 1848 and located to the rear of the field house, is the second major observatory in the D.C. area. (The Naval Observatory *(see page 57)* is the other.)

The university's president from 1874 to 1882 was Father Patrick J. Healy, the first black man to head a major white university. Healy, the son of an Irish immigrant and a mulatto mother, was born in Georgia. Stately Healy Hall on the Georgetown campus, a beautiful building in Flemish Renaissance style, was the result of Father Healy's endeavours. Georgetown's School of Foreign Service has produced many top U.S. diplomatic figures. President Bill Clinton attended Georgetown, and numerous presidential offspring have also attended.

51

Also in Georgetown is the ★★ **Dumbarton Oaks** ⓭ mansion with its 10 acres (4 hectares) of formal gardens. During World War II, key meetings were held at Dumbarton Oaks which led to the Manhattan Project, the military program to develop the atomic bomb. In 1944, preliminary discussions were held here between Russian, British, American, and Chinese delegates, leading to the founding of the United Nations at San Francisco in 1945.

When Georgetown was first settled, the land on which the mansion and garden now stand was granted to pioneer Ninian Beall, who named his bequest the Rock of Dumbarton after a landmark in his native Scotland. The central Federal-style house, situated on the crest of a wooded valley overlooking Rock Creek, was built about 1801 by William Dorsey, a judge. South Carolinian John C. Calhoun and his brother James purchased the house in 1822, when John was serving as Secretary of War. He later became Speaker of the House of Representatives and chief spokesman for the southern cause in the great debates on slavery in the 1840s.

Dumbarton Oaks gates

The house and grounds were bought in 1920 by Foreign Service Officer Robert Woods Bliss and his wife, Mildred Barnes Bliss, who expanded the estate considerably and created the beautiful gardens we see today. Especially noteworthy is the Music Room, which was added to the house in 1929. There you will find a 16th-century chimney piece, an 18th-century parquet floor, and a ceiling painted in 16th-century style.

In 1940 the Blisses conveyed the house, gardens, and a considerable collection of pre-Columbian and Byzantine art and artifacts to Harvard University, which established here the Dumbarton Oaks Research Library and Collection (April to October, daily 2pm–6pm; November to March, 2pm–5pm). Entering the house from 32nd Street, you start your visit with these collections.

Take a stroll around the luxurious gardens, designed by Mildred Bliss and landscape artist, Beatrice Farrand, which include ten pools and nine fountains. The pathways wind through the many different gardens, each separated by a wall or by hills, creating a sense of both solitude and of grandeur in the design.

Antiquities at Dumbarton Oaks

The estate is also associated with leading musical figures of the 20th century: the Polish composer and pianist Ignace Paderewski, Polish harpsichordist Wanda Landowska, the Spanish soprano Lucrezia Bori, and, above all, Russian composer Igor Stravinsky, who composed his Dumbarton Oaks Symphony for the Bliss's 30th wedding anniversary.

A greater architectural contrast to the Old Stone House could hardly be found than in **Tudor Place** 44, at 1644 31st Street, N.W. (tours, preferably by prior notice: Tuesday to Friday 10am, 11:30am, 1pm, 2:30pm; Saturday, every hour 10am–3pm; tel: (202) 965-0400). The first buildings here were built around 1797 for a wealthy tobacco merchant, Francis Lowndes. In 1805, Tudor Place was purchased by Thomas Peter and his wife, Martha, the granddaughter of George Washington's wife, with money inherited from the first president.

Peter asked William Thornton, architect of the Capitol, to design the main part of the house, incorporating the two small existing buildings. The result is considered one of the prime examples of Federal architecture in Washington. Even if you are unable to join a tour, you can visit the garden (Monday to Saturday 1–4pm) and view the building from outside.

Indoor mall on M Street

Aside from the university and lovely residential streets, Georgetown is best known for its shops. Most of these are located on the main thoroughfares of M Street and Wisconsin Avenue. Reaching Georgetown can be difficult, however. Parking here is difficult, and the nearest Metrorail stop is Foggy Bottom, about a 20-minute walk from the main shopping area on M Street. Several bus routes pass through the area, however.

Georgetown has no department stores, but there are many small shops selling antiques, jewelry, women's and men's fashions, books, and gifts of all kinds. It is also very lively at night, with restaurants, bars, and clubs.

mbassy Row and Upper Northwest

upont Circle – Adams Morgan – Phillips Collection
Anderson House – Woodrow Wilson House – Kalo-
ama Circle – Embassy Row – National Cathedral –
ational Zoo *See map, pages 48–9*

his route takes you through some of Washington's most
egant residential areas, where many of the foreign em-
assies and ambassadors' residences are located, as well
s some charming small museums.

upont Circle **45** lay on the outskirts of the original City
Washington, in a section known as "The Slashes." Now
's a rather chic, bohemian area, the D.C. equivalent to
ew York's Greenwich Village. During the last quarter of
e 19th century, the location became a prime target for
ealthy real estate investors, as the massive public works
rojects of the 1870s began to transform Washington into
fashionable capital city.

The circle was named in honor of Admiral Samuel F.
uPont, who commanded the ironclads (the first armored
arships) in a failed attempt to take Charleston, S.C. in
863. Its centerpiece, a large graceful fountain, was de-
gned by Daniel Chester French who also sculpted the
incoln statue in the Lincoln Memorial.

Nearby are the homes of the barons of the turn-of-the-
entury Gilded Age. After the Stock Market Crash of 1929,
ost of the fortunes which built these mansions abruptly
isappeared, and since then, the cost of running them has
ky-rocketed. Most survive today either as headquarters
r national organizations or societies, or as embassies.

Embassy Row

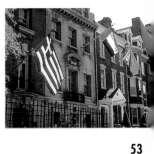

53

Dupont Circle fountain

The **Patterson House** at 15 Dupont Circle, for instance, is now the headquarters of a prominent womens' organization, the Washington Club. Previously it was the home of socialite Cissy Patterson, who for a time owned the *Washington Times-Herald* and who virtually created the "society page" as a political force. A typical guest-list for Cissy's own "bashes" at the mansion would include actress Ethel Barrymore, FBI chief J. Edgar Hoover, union official John L. Lewis, and newspaper magnate William Randolph Hearst.

A fortune made in beer was the basis for the construction of the **Heurich Mansion** 46 at 1307 New Hampshire Ave, N.W., one block south of the Circle (Tuesday to Saturday 1–4pm). This 31-room brownstone structure serves today as home of the Historical Society of Washington. In 1892 Heurich built a brewery on the present site of the Kennedy Center, which operated until 1956.

A visit to Dupont Circle would not be complete without browsing in ★ **Kramerbooks** (1517 Connecticut Avenue, open Sunday to Thursday 7:30am–1am; Friday and Saturday 24 hours). In business since 1976, Kramers anticipated the trend for the "bookcafé." The café serves breakfast, lunch, and dinner.

If you go north from Dupont Circle up Connecticut Avenue and turn right on Columbia Road after the Washington Hilton, you'll enter the **Adams-Morgan** 4 district. Since the 1970s, this has been one of the city's most diverse residential districts and the heart of its Latin American community. Restaurants and carry-outs abound, offering paella, chorizo, sangria, black beans and other latino favorites.

The original "bookcafé"

Patterson House on Dupont Circle

If you're more interested in historic mansions, walk northwest from Dupont Circle up Massachusetts Avenue, popularly known as ★ **Embassy Row**. At 2000 Massachusetts you can see the **Blaine Mansion**, now a National Historic Landmark. This was built in 1882 for James Gillespie Blaine, a prominent Republican. The building was later purchased by inventor George Westinghouse.

At 2020 Massachusetts Avenue you'll see the Art Nouveau architecture of the **Walsh-McLean Mansion**, today the Indonesian Embassy. The mansion was built in 1903 by an Irishman, Thomas Francis Walsh, a self-made man who made his fortune in the Gold Rush.

At the northwest corner of 21st and O streets you'll find one of the more important, though lesser known, art collections in the city, the ★★ **Phillips Collection 48**. In 1921 Duncan Phillips and his artist-wife, Marjorie, opened their home to the public as a museum – the country's first public modern art gallery. The collection focusses on French Impressionists and Post-Impressionists, but there are Old Masters and American modernists as well. Among works on display are Cézanne's 1877 *Self-Portrait*, Renoir's *Luncheon of the Boating Party*, and a larger number of paintings by Pierre Bonnard.

55

The **Cosmos Club**, at 2121 Massachusetts, is a meeting place of distinguished men (predominately) in science, literature, and the fine arts.

Cosmos Club

On the other side of the street, at No. 2118, is the ★ **Anderson House 49** (Tuesday to Saturday 1–4pm), the headquarters of the Society of the Cincinnati, an organization founded in 1783 by a group of officers of the Continental Army before their demobilization after the Revolutionary War. Membership was limited to officers and their eldest male descendants. A visit to the house is very worthwhile, to see the beautiful furnishings as well as the Revolutionary War memorabilia.

Garden of the Textile Museum

Continue up Massachusetts Avenue and turn right on to 24th Street, and right again on to S Street. The **Textile Museum 50** (Monday to Saturday 10am–5pm, Sunday 1–5pm) at 2320 S Street is unique in the plethora of museums in Washington. It contains pre-Columbian, Egyptian, and Islamic textiles, Oriental carpets, and the world's finest collection of Peruvian weavings.

Enjoying the summer

A bit further east on S Street is the **Woodrow Wilson House** (Tuesday to Sunday 10am–4pm). Wilson led the country through World War I, and in 1918 proposed the creation of a League of Nations which would promote world peace by resolving international conflicts. After serving two terms as president, Wilson, unlike most presidents, decided to remain in Washington. Today his house is a museum with much memorabilia and many portraits.

Fountain at Decatur Terrace

If you have time, walk further down S Street a block or so to **Decatur Terrace**, an artful stone staircase going down the hill to Decatur Place and ornamented with an elaborate fountain. This idyllic spot is known locally as the Spanish Steps.

Walking north on 24th Street toward ★ **Kalorama Circle ㉛**, you'll pass through one of the finest residential districts in the city, home to many more embassies, and will be able to enjoy beautiful views of Rock Creek Park. Look out for the **French Embassy** at 2221 Kalorama Road, a fine example of a Tudor-style country manor. The diplomat and poet Joel Barlow bought property in this area in 1805 and named it Kalorama Heights, after the Greek word meaning "fine view." The neighborhood is noted for its Georgian Revival houses and was, at various times, home to presidents Taft, Wilson, Harding, and Hoover.

Tudor-style French Embassy

Continuing up Embassy Row, you'll see on your right the minaret of the **Islamic Center ㉜**. This is a functioning Muslim mosque and welcomes Muslims from all countries. The interior boasts a rich design, carpeted with Persian rugs and a pulpit inlaid with ivory and ebony. The mosque faces Mecca and prayer services are held at noon on Friday. Non-Muslims are invited to witness the services, but must take off their shoes before entering.

Islamic Center

The mosque overlooks ★ **Rock Creek Park ㉝**, the enormous green space surrounding the tiny Rock Creek, which flows directly through the District into the Potomac near the Kennedy Center. During the early 1800s, the creek was navigable all the way up to P Street in Georgetown. Numerous mills operated on its banks, making use of the ower of the flowing stream. The mills' importance diminished with the construction of the Chesapeake and Ohio Canal, and the remains of a few mills can still be seen. The park is an ideal place for jogging, hiking, biking, or horse-back riding.

Continuing up Massachusetts Avenue you will pass a **Statue of Winston Churchill** ❺❹ on your left. This was dedicated on April 9, 1966 on the third anniversary of the granting of honorary U.S. citizenship to Sir Winston. Just behind the statue is the British ambassador's residence. The building, which served initially as both embassy and residence, was designed in the 1920s by Sir Edwin Luytens, who also designed the British Viceroy's Palace in New Delhi. By 1950, the building had become too small and a new embassy was built next door.

Statue of Churchill on Massachusetts Avenue

The ★ **Naval Observatory** ❺❺ (evening tours Monday on first come, first served basis; gates open at 7:30pm) is well worth a visit. Founded in 1830 as a Depot of Charts and Instruments, the Naval Observatory is one of the oldest scientific agencies in the country. John Quincy Adams, the sixth president, proposed the creation of a "lighthouse in the sky," and it was originally located in the area known as Foggy Bottom because of the mist and fog coming from the Potomac River. In spite of these impediments, it was here that astronomer Asaph Hall discovered the two moons of Mars, Phobos and Deimos in 1877.

The Observatory, which moved to its present location in 1893, also operates the atomic clocks which keep accurate time for the entire country. On your tour you will see both the clocks and some of the Observatory's telescopes. On a clear night, you will be allowed to view the skies from one of these. The official residence of the vice president is also located in the grounds of the Observatory.

Continuing up Massachusetts Avenue, the massive ★★ **Washington National Cathedral** ❺❻ (April to September, Monday to Friday 10am–9pm, Saturday 10am–4:30pm, Sunday 12:30–4:30pm; October to March, Monday to Saturday 10am–4:30pm, Sunday 12:30–4:30pm) can be spotted long before you reach Wisconsin Avenue. A right turn on Wisconsin will take you to the entrance.

West Front of the National Cathedral

Mount St. Albans, site of the magnificent cathedral, is the highest point in the city, 676ft (206m) above sea level. George Washington first proposed building a "national" cathedral in the city. When, in 1891, it was decided to build an Episcopal cathedral, the founders decided to make it a "witness to Christian unity" and the national cathedral that the L'Enfant Plan had envisaged. The site they chose was then considered rather daring because of its great distance from the center of the city. But the site

Cathedral nave

Stained glass in a side chapel

The big day arrives

is an impressive one, and today the cathedral can be seen from as far away as the banks of the Potomac River.

Built in English Gothic style in the same manner as medieval churches, stone upon stone with no structural steel but supported by flying buttresses, bosses, and vaults the cathedral is 514ft (157m) long and contains more than 200 stained-glass windows. Although it is the seat of the Episcopal diocese, it also serves as a "great church for national purposes." Formally known as the Cathedral Church of Saint Peter and Paul, it is the second largest church in the United States and the sixth largest church in the world

The cornerstone was laid on September 29, 1907 by President Theodore Roosevelt. During construction, sections of the building came into use as they were completed over the years, many funerals of major public figures, such as presidents Truman and Eisenhower, have been held here. The final stone was set in place, in a ceremony attended by President George Bush, in September 1990.

The church is indeed immense. The distance from the back of the nave to the high altar is one-tenth of a mile (160 m). Special attention should be paid to the beautiful ★ **West Rose Window** by Rowan LeCompte. The window contains over 10,500 pieces of glass, depicting in an abstract manner the creation theme of Genesis, "Let there be light."

Also not to be missed is the **Space Window**, commemorating the flight of Apollo XI. The design depicts the trajectory of a circling spacecraft traveling from the Earth to the Moon; in the middle is a sliver of Moon rock brought back from one of the Apollo missions. A little further toward the front is the sarcophagus of Woodrow Wil-

son, the only president buried in the cathedral. Much of the construction of the cathedral took place during the Wilson presidency, and Wilson would frequently visit the construction site.

A statue of George Washington is in the first bay, near the entrance, and another bay has a bronze statue of Lincoln. At the Crossing, where the nave meets the choir, you'll see the Canterbury Pulpit, made of stone from Canterbury Cathedral in England. It was from this pulpit that Martin Luther King spoke on March 31, 1968; this was his last Sunday sermon before his assassination four days later. Indira Gandhi also spoke from this pulpit.

In the crypt is the Bethlehem Chapel, the oldest part of the cathedral near the cornerstone. Admiral George Dewey, the Spanish-American War hero, is buried here. Passing on to the Chapel of St. Joseph of Arimathea, you will see the wrought-iron gate which leads to the cathedral's columbarium, where Helen Keller and her teacher, Anne Sullivan Macy, are interred. If time allows, take the elevator up to the Pilgrim Observation Gallery to get an excellent view of the city.

Reredos of the High Altar

The grounds of the cathedral were designed by Frederick Law Olmsted, Jr. Before leaving, be sure to visit the ★ **Bishop's Garden** on the southern side of the building, modelled on a medieval walled garden with roses, perennials, boxwood, herbs, and flowers. A greenhouse (Monday to Saturday 9am–5pm, Sunday 10am–5pm) sells annuals, perennials, and herbs; dried herbs and gift items can be purchased at the herb cottage. A book and gift shop is also located in the basement of the cathedral.

Bishop's Garden with gazebo

Adjacent to the cathedral is the **St. Albans School for Boys**, a private college preparatory school modelled on the English "public schools." St. Albans has become the preferred destination for the male offspring of the area's elite, including the sons and grandsons of Franklin Roosevelt, Katherine Graham (owner of the *Washington Post*), and President George Bush.

A few minutes' drive east from the cathedral is the entrance to the ★★ **National Zoological Park** **57** on Connecticut Avenue (grounds open May to mid September, daily 8am–8pm; mid September to April, daily 8am–6pm; buildings open daily 9am–4:30pm; zoo closed December 25). Enclosures on the 160-acre (65-hectare) site are designed to house the animals in settings resembling their native habitat. The two giant pandas, given by China in 1972, are justly famous, but visit the Great Ape House and, especially, the Great Flight Cage in which the birds fly around you. During the summer, there is a sea lion demonstration at 11:30am. The best time to visit is in the morning; many animals take a siesta in the afternoon heat.

Lions at the Zoo

Alexandria's Old Town Square

Additional Sights

Further away from the main tourist areas of Northwest Washington are a number of important sights. Some, such as Arlington National Cemetery, are generally thronged with visitors; others, like Hillwood, are not easy to visit, but are well worth the effort. Here are the best, described in alphabetical order.

★★ **Alexandria, Virginia** was a booming commercial town long before the establishment of the nation's capital. Founded in 1749 by Scottish merchants, Alexandria was a major tobacco port and there was easy access for boats traveling up from Chesapeake Bay. Many of the leading families of the American republic came from Alexandria. George Mason, author of the Bill of Rights, lived in the area, as did the Washingtons. The Lee family of Virginia, one of whom signed the Declaration of Independence, also hailed from Alexandria.

After independence, the town was considered as a potential capital city. Ironically, it was George Washington – concerned that he might appear biased toward his home state – who quelled such talk. Alexandria and neighboring Arlington were ceded back to the state of Virginia in 1846.

A walk through Alexandria's Old Town gives a feel for what life was like in colonial days. Start your tour at the Lyceum, on the corner of Washington and Prince Streets, a graceful example of Greek Revival architecture and now a museum. Walk east on Prince Street, make a right on Royal Street, and take the next left on Duke Street. This will take you to the Old Presbyterian Meeting House at 321 South Fairfax Street. The church has many associations with the Freemasons of the Revolutionary War period; Washington attended Masonic ceremonies here.

Walk north up Fairfax Street to the Stabler-Leadbeater Apothecary Shop. Pills, tablets, and capsules were made up here by the druggist, the Quaker Edward Stabler. The customers included the Lee and the Washingtons for several generations. The apothecary, as well as many other stores in the area, was ransacked in 1814 by British troops on their way to Washington. Continue on Fairfax past the Ramsay House, built in 1724 for

Robert E Lee's Boyhood Home
Lee - Fendall House
Oronoco St.
Princess St.
Queen St.
Washington St.
St Asaph St.
Pitt St.
Royal St.
Fairfax St.
Lee St.
General Henry Lee's Home
Cameron St.
Carlyle House
Tavern Square
Market Square
Ramsay House
King St.
Stabler–Leadbeater Apothecary Shop
Prince St.
The Lyceum
Duke St.
St Mary's Church
ALEXANDRIA
N
0   180 m
0   200 yds
Old Presbyterian Meeting House

William Ramsay, a young Scotsman who became one of the town's most illustrious founding fathers. Today the building serves as the Visitors' Center.

Continuing up Fairfax Street, you'll also pass the Carlyle House, an unusual old country-style house and an outstanding example of colonial Georgian architecture. Turn left on Cameron Street. On the next block on your left is Gadsby's Tavern. The older, smaller building is from 1770; the larger, adjoining building was built in 1792 as the City Hotel. The register of distinguished guests reads like a "Who's Who" of the American Revolution: George Washington, John Adams, John Quincy Adams, Thomas Jefferson, as well as the Marquis de Lafayette.

Walking further on Cameron Street, on your right you will find the home of "Lighthorse Harry" Lee, a Revolutionary War general and father of Robert E. Lee, and, crossing Washington Street, the elegant Christ Church. George Washington was an original pewholder in the church and Robert E. Lee, the Confederate leader, later attended services here.

Walk three blocks north on North Washington Street and you will come to the boyhood home of Robert E. Lee, at 607 Oronoco Street. Across the street is the Lee-Fendall House, another Lee family home.

Pews at Christ Church

61

The **Anacostia Museum** (1901 Fort Place, S.E.; daily 10am–5pm) documents the African-American history and culture of Washington, D.C. and the southern states. It is located across the Anacostia River in the Southeast section of Washington. The museum maintains continually changing exhibits which are often of great interest, but has no permanent exhibits.

A visit to the museum could be followed by a visit to **Cedar Hill** (1411 W Street, S.E.; May to September, daily 9am–5pm; October to April, 9am–4pm), the home of abolitionist and former slave Frederick Douglass. Douglass (1817–95) had been absolutely irrepressible in his attempts to ensure that the country's political leaders kept their promises to the country's black citizens. A runaway slave, he finally settled in Washington in 1871 and became editor of the *New National*. He served as Marshal of the District of Columbia from 1877 to 1881.

The house was dedicated as a memorial to Douglass in 1922, and has been faithfully restored to how it was in Douglass's time. There is no Metrorail stop in the vicinity, which is best reached by car.

Arlington National Cemetery (April to September, daily 8am–7pm; October to March, 8am–5pm), just across Memorial Bridge from the Lincoln Memorial, is one of more than 100 national cemeteries in the country.

Arlington National Cemetery

The 612-acre (248-hectare) plot was at one time owned by Mary Randolph Custis, a relative of George Washington. She married Lieutenant Robert E. Lee, who later became Commander-in-Chief of Confederate forces during the Civil War.

At the beginning of the Civil War, the strategic heights of Arlington overlooking the capital were occupied by federal troops from Washington, and Arlington House was turned into the headquarters of the Army of the Potomac. In 1864, Arlington House and its estate were confiscated by the government from the Lee family, on a legal technicality. Because of the desperate need for more cemeteries in which to bury soldiers, part of the estate was set aside for that purpose. By the end of the Civil War more than 16,000 headstones dotted the Arlington landscape.

A Freedman's Village for freed black slaves had also been established on the estate in June 1863 and remained in existence there until 1893. More than 3,800 African-Americans are buried at Arlington, in graves marked "civilian" or "citizen."

Eternal Flame at the grave of John F. Kennedy

Of special note in the cemetery is the gravesite of John F. Kennedy, situated just below the crest of the hill of Arlington House. With him are buried his wife Jackie, his infant son Patrick, and an unnamed infant daughter. The gravesite is marked by an Eternal Flame. Kennedy's brother, Robert F. Kennedy, is buried close by.

From there you can walk up an adjacent hill to the Tomb of the Unknowns. An Honor Guard from the First Battle Group, Third Infantry Regiment, the oldest infantry unit in the United States, always stands guard in front of the tomb. The impressive changing of the guard ceremony occurs every half hour during the summer months, and hourly during the rest of the year. The tomb contains the remains of unknown military personnel from World War I, World War II, the Korean conflict, and the Vietnam conflict.

Burial at Arlington is restricted to members of the Armed Forces who die in active service; retired members, those who performed honorable military service and also held elective office of the federal government; and their spouse, widow or widower, or minor child. Famous Americans buried here include Pierre L'Enfant, jurist Oliver Wendell Holmes, Rear Adm. Richard E. Byrd, Lt. Gen. Claire L. Chennault, Gen. George C. Marshall, and Gen. Omar Bradley. Some 240,000 people have been buried at Arlington, and the number continues to grow each week.

Iwo Jima Memorial

Just north of the cemetery is the Marine Corps War Memorial, more familiarly known as the ★ **Iwo Jima Memorial**. The 78-ft-long (24-m) sculpture, designed by Horace W. Peaslee and cast by Felix de Weldon, is the largest bronze statue ever cast. It is based on a staged photograph taken by Joseph Rosenthal after the battle or the Japanese island of Iwo Jima in March 1945, of four Marines and one sailor raising the American flag on Mount Suribachi. By order of the president, the flag at the Marine Corps War Memorial is always flying. The memorial is a short walk from Rosslyn Station, on the Orange and Blue Lines.

National Shrine

The ★ **Basilica of the National Shrine of the Immaculate Conception**, the biggest Roman Catholic place of worship in the United States, is at 4th Street and Michigan Avenue, N.E. (April to October, daily 7am–7pm; November to March, 7am–6pm) and can be reached by Metrorail on the Red Line (Brookland-CUA stop). Inspired by elements from Byzantine, Romanesque, and modern architecture, the building is decorated with mosaics, stained glass, and sculpture. The cornerstone for this tremendous structure was laid in 1920. It can seat up to 6,000 people and inside there are 55 chapels.

★ **Great Falls Park** (daily, 7am–90 minutes after dusk) is located at the point where the Potomac River falls 76ft (23m) over a succession of enormous boulders. It's especially impressive after a heavy rainfall, with many tons of water flooding through the Mather Gorge.

Here you can also see the results of the initial attempt by George Washington to make the Potomac River navigable. Look out for the remains of this Patowmack Canal, which was lauded in the journals of the day as a great engineering feat. The canal was completed in 1802 and operated until 1820.

Great Falls is a lovely area to visit, and is full of wildlife, including osprey, beavers, deer, rabbits, and foxes. It can be reached on the Virginia side via George Washington

Great Falls Park

The gardens of Hillwood

Parkway (which runs past Arlington Cemetery) a Georgetown Pike. Or you can visit the Falls from t Maryland side, although since there's no bridge, it mea taking an alternative route, from Georgetown. On Maryland side you can see Great Falls Tavern, now a m seum. You'll also be able to go out on a walkway acro Olmsted Island and walk over rivulets of the falls, b fore arriving at the Overlook. You can also have a clos look at the C&O Canal; rides on the canal boats dep from the Visitors Center at the tavern.

Do not, however, attempt to have a closer look at falls themselves, as the rocks can be slippery and ma reckless visitors have lost their lives here.

★ **Hillwood** (4155 Linnean Avenue, N.W.; Tuesday Saturday by appointment only; tel: (202) 686-8500) well off the beaten track for tourists and difficult to fir but definitely worth a visit. Located on grounds ove looking Rock Creek Park north of the zoo, it can only reached by car. Comprising 25 acres (10 hectares), Hi wood was formerly the estate of Marjorie Merriweath Post, heiress to the Post breakfast cereal fortune. In 19 Mrs. Post married Joseph Davies, the U.S. ambassad to the Soviet Union, and spent 18 months there.

Over the years, she amassed the largest collection of i perial Russian art objects outside Russia. The Russian c lection includes state portraits of czars and czarinas, as w as grand furnishings that once embellished palaces a churches. There are 90 objects from the Fabergé worksho including some of the legendary Easter eggs made for t imperial family. Hillwood is also known for its 18th-ce tury furniture, Sèvres porcelain, and Beauvais tapestrie

The well-tended grounds include a Japanese-style ga den, where a waterfall cascades down a steep hill.

The ★ **Kenilworth Aquatic Gardens** (Kenilworth A enue and Douglas Street, N.E.; open daily during daylig hours) consist of 44 small display ponds containing w ter lilies and lotus, water hyacinth, bamboo and other w ter plants. The 700-acre (283-hectare) Kenilworth Pa includes the Aquatic Gardens and has fresh-water tic wetlands, mud flats, bottomland forest, river channels, ve nal pools, freshwater streams, and a developed spring. is about a 10-minute walk from Deanwood Station the Orange Line, but is most safely reached by car.

★★ **Mount Vernon**, the home of George Washington, located 16 miles (26km) south of Washington on the Vi ginia side of the Potomac down the George Washingt Memorial Parkway (April to August, daily 8am–5pr March, September, October, 9am–5pm; November

Hands-on at Mount Vernon

ebruary, 9am–4pm). It is not accessible by Metrorail.

Start your visit at the mansion itself, which was built
n 1735. The Mount Vernon Ladies' Association provides
nformation about each room of the house, which contains
many original furnishings and is painted in the bright hues
sed in the 18th century. During the spring and summer,
t is often very crowded, so try to arrive early. The build-
ng's exterior is covered in wooden shingles made to look
ke the rusticated stone commonly found in Italian Re-
aissance architecture. From the mansion, whose veranda
verlooks the Potomac, proceed to the many outbuildings
long the north and south lanes, including the salthouse,
he spinning house, the coachhouse, a stablehouse, and the
laves' quarters (Washington owned over 300 slaves).
here are also two gardens near the house.

Continue down the hill to the tomb of George and
Martha Washington. There you will also find a slave bur-
al ground. A museum on the grounds has Washington
amily memorabilia.

Mount Vernon

The **National Arboretum**'s (daily 8am–5pm; closed
December 25) beautiful 444-acre (180-hectare) spread is
a short drive northeast of the Capitol. Visitor entrances
re located on New York Avenue and on R Street, N.E.
The grounds encompass an array of gardens, horticul-
ural collections, and historical monuments. It is best to
isit by car, as the arboretum is not accessible by Metro-
ail. Inside, there are places to park throughout the vast
omplex, so you can stop and walk around at will.

Among the plant collections are a grove of trees rep-
esenting every state in the Union; a display of Chinese,
apanese, and North American-styled pot trees; and the
vorld's most complete living collection of boxwoods. In
eason, you can also view the beautiful azalea collection,
olorful hollies and magnolia trees, and a collection of na-
ive plant collections from the eastern United States.

Arrayed in front of a reflecting pool are 22 of the orig-
nal sandstone Corinthian columns that stood on the east
ortico of the Capitol until its renovation in 1957.

National Arboretum

The **Pentagon**, powerhouse of the U.S. defense establishment, is one of the world's biggest and most impos-
ng office buildings (Monday to Friday, tours every half
our, 9:30am–3:30pm). Completed in 1943, it has three
imes the floor space of the Empire State Building in
New York. There are presently, after considerable downsizing, approximately 23,000 employees working in the
Pentagon. The building contains 17.5 miles (28km) of
corridors, but it takes only seven minutes to walk be-
ween any two points in the building. It is easily accessi-
le, as it has its own Metrorail stop on the Blue Line.

Excursions in Maryland

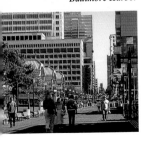

Baltimore Harbor

Baltimore

In contrast to the administrative center of Washington, Baltimore is a seafaring and industrial town, one of the biggest seaports on the East Coast, and only 41 miles (66km) away (about an hour's drive).

Recently ★★ **Baltimore Harbor** has been transformed into a major tourist stop, with shops, restaurants, and entertainment galore. You can take a water taxi (day pass available) to visit the various stops on the waterfront. There you will also find the National Aquarium, the Maryland Science Center, and the Museum of Industry.

Baltimore is the location of historic ★★ **Fort McHenry**, where the unsuccessful British bombardment in 1814 inspired Francis Scott Key to write the poem which became the U.S. national anthem, "The Star-Spangled Banner". This star-shaped brick fort is still standing, with exhibits depicting life at a military fort in 1814.

Baltimore is also where the great poet and novelist, Edgar Allan Poe, began his career. The **Edgar Allan Poe House and Museum** (Monday to Friday, noon–5pm) contains exhibits and artifacts relating to Poe's life and work. Legendary baseball player Babe Ruth is generally associated with New York, but his home is really Baltimore, and the **Babe Ruth Birthplace** is a must for baseball fans. For railroad buffs there's the B&O Railroad Museum or for seafarers, the frigate U.S.S. *Constellation*, first launched in 1797, which lies in dock down on Pier I. Combine a trip to the *Constellation* with a visit to the fine **Baltimore Maritime Museum** at Pier III. Art lovers will enjoy the enormous collections of the **Walters Art Gallery** and the ★ **Baltimore Museum of Art**.

In addition there are a number of fine old mansions. The **Carroll Mansion** was the home of Charles Carroll, a signer of the Declaration of Independence. **Mount Clare Museum House**, Baltimore's only pre-Revolutionary War mansion, is also worth a visit.

Annapolis

A visit to Annapolis, Maryland gives a good picture of what life was like in early colonial times. Annapolis is the capital of Maryland, and for a time the Continental Congress also met here. You can visit another home of Charles Carroll, or the **Hammond-Harwood House**, an outstanding example of colonial architecture. Equally fine is the **William Paca House**, built in 1763–5 for this revolutionary leader. To dine in a colonial setting, go to **Reynolds Tavern**, an authentic 18th-century tavern in the heart of historic Annapolis.

Annapolis is also the location of the **United States**

68

Naval Academy, the prestigious undergraduate college of the U.S. Navy. The Visitors' Center (March to November, 9am–5pm; December to February, 9am–4pm) should be your first stop, to find out what is open to visitors and to get the times of the regular guided tours of the facility. Also stop to visit the ★ **U.S. Naval Academy Museum** (Monday to Saturday, 9am–5pm; Sunday 1am–5pm), with its collection of 108 ship and boat models of the sailing ship era dating from 1650 to 1850.

Frederick

Frederick is a small, picturesque town in eastern Maryland. In the center of town is **Courthouse Square**, surrounded by many distinguished Federal row houses. You can see the law offices of Supreme Court Chief Justice Roger Brooke Taney and Francis Scott Key, the author of "The Star-Spangled Banner".

The town also has a lot of Civil War history. This is the home of Barbara Fritchie, the 95-year-old woman whose refusal to take down the flag when Confederate forces entered the town was immortalized in a poem by John Greenleaf Whittier: "'Shoot, if you must, this old gray head, But spare your country's flag,' she said." The Confederate general, "Stonewall" Jackson, instructed his troops, "'Who touches a hair of yon gray head, Dies like a dog! March on!' he said." The **Fritchie House** on West Patrick Street, now a museum, has been reconstructed using original furnishings and building materials.

In **Kemp Hall** the Maryland legislature convened in 1861 to vote on whether the state should secede from the Union. Confederate sympathizers were in the majority, but Unionists delayed the decision long enough for federal troops to arrive and arrest the rebels. Maryland was the only southern state not to join the Confederate cause.

Federal houses in Frederick

Whimsical window

Courthouse Square

69

Bloody Lane

*Civil War monument
at Antietam*

*Beach at Sandy Point, near the
Chesapeake Bay Bridge*

Antietam

★ **Antietam National Battlefield** is located near Sharpsburg in western Maryland, just north of Harper's Ferry, West Virginia. The Battle of Antietam on September 17, 1862 was the bloodiest day of the Civil War. Federal losses totaled 12,410 and the Confederates lost 10,700 men. Confederate General Robert E. Lee's thrust into the north had been turned back, at least for the time being. For President Abraham Lincoln, this victory signalled that the time had come to issue the Emancipation Proclamation, which freed the slaves in areas rebelling against the Union.

You can visit the battlefield on foot, but be sure to go into the Visitors' Center first for an orientation. Some of the more famous highlights of the battle were the fight at Bloody Lane (Sunken Road) and at the Cornfield. Climb the watchtower to get a better overview of the field.

Beaches

Visitors who enjoy the sand and the sea should remember that when in Washington, you're never too far from the water. During the summer months, though, be prepared for the crowds heading to the Atlantic beaches of the ★★ **Delmarva peninsula** (formed by parts of Delaware, Maryland, and Virginia). Weekends are the most congested, especially the Memorial Day (end of May) and Labor Day (end of August) holiday weekends, and traffic leading to the Chesapeake Bay Bridges can be fierce.

Fortunately, there are plenty of beaches to choose from. Some of the quieter ones are in Delaware, such as Bethany Beach and Fenwick Island State Park, but there are fewer motels here than in busy Rehoboth or in Ocean City, further south across the border with Maryland.

Excursions in Virginia

Williamsburg

If you really want "living" history, then the place to go is ★★★ **Colonial Williamsburg**. About a 3-hour drive from Washington, the whole town is organized around keeping the old city, some of which dates back to the 18th century, exactly as it was then. During the 1930s, philanthropist John D. Rockefeller, Jr., committed himself to making Williamsburg a living monument, and provided funds for rebuilding many of the historic buildings that had been destroyed over the years. With the help of historical records, they were reconstructed in their original locations and to their original designs.

Many townsfolk today are employed to maintain the activities of an 18th-century village. Merchants sell their wares, craftspeople ply their trades, and patriots talk of plans of revolution. It may sound corny, but it is done so well that it is very convincing.

Williamsburg patriot

The town became the capital of the Virginia colony in 1699, replacing the capital at Jamestown, which had been the first permanent English settlement in the New World. The new capital was named in honor of King William III. After independence, it served for a time as capital of the Commonwealth of Virginia, one of the original 13 states of the Union. It is the location of the College of William and Mary, the second oldest college in America, founded in 1693.

Take a walk along the central **Duke of Gloucester Street** and its side streets. There are 88 original and hundreds of replicated colonial buildings here. The **Capitol** building is a reconstruction of the one built by Henry Cary in 1705 and destroyed in 1881. With the help of historical records, the building has been refurnished as it was in that period. The Capitol houses the re-created House of Burgesses. The gentlemen of this House sat in the oldest representative assembly in the New World; here, revolutionary leader Patrick Henry gave some of his most stirring speeches, although not his most famous one, which concluded, "I know not what course others may take; but as for me, give me liberty, or give me death."

Next to the Capitol is the **Public Gaol** (jail). Among the more important prisoners to be jailed here were 15 henchmen of the famous pirate, Blackbeard. Many of the prisoners were, however, simply men who couldn't pay their debts. Also on Duke of Gloucester Street, you'll find Raleigh Tavern, a reconstruction that interprets the lively social life of the colonial capital.

Walk down Palace Green to the **Governor's Palace**. This is a reconstruction of the 1722 palace of the royal

Governor's Palace

The silversmith's shop

Stock character

Old-time transportation

governor replete with elegant woodwork, furnishings, and an ornamental display of firearms. The palace was also the scene of festive occasions; Governor Alexander Spotswood, a mentor of George Washington, spoke of playing host here to 200 people one evening.

Go back to Duke of Gloucester Street and walk west to the **Bruton Parish Church**. Completed about 1712, the elegant cruciform brick church has held services ever since. Attendees included Patrick Henry, Thomas Jefferson, and George Washington.

At the end of Duke of Gloucester Street, the ★ **College of William and Mary** has several interesting sights, such as the Wren Building. Destroyed by Union forces who entered the city to prevent Confederate snipers from using it as cover, the building was restored in the 1930s. The first floor of the Wren Building is maintained as a Colonial Williamsburg exhibition. Historians cannot agree whether Sir Christopher Wren, the royal architect who built St. Paul's Cathedral in London, designed the building. Wren's office may have drawn up the plans, but statements which indicate that he himself designed the building are disputed.

The brick **President's House**, on the north side of the college yard, is one of the few Georgian buildings that remained intact even through the Civil War. The building was also designed by Henry Cary, who built the Capitol. In 1781, the house sheltered the British General Cornwallis shortly before his defeat at Yorktown, the decisive battle of the Revolutionary War.

Visitors to Williamsburg must purchase tickets at the Visitors' Center. The passes on offer allow access for a whole day or more to the town's many buildings.

From Williamsburg, take the opportunity to visit neighboring **Busch Gardens**, a 360-acre (146-hectare) amuse-nent park filled with live shows and over 35 fantastic rides, ncluding the double-looping Loch Ness Monster and the ravity-defying Drachen Fire roller coasters.

Just a few miles from Williamsburg on the banks of he James River are **Jamestown Settlement** and **James-own Island**, where in 1607 a few hardy souls carved ut of the wilderness the first permanent English settle-nent in the New World. Also nearby is **Yorktown**, where General Cornwallis surrendered to General Washington.

redericksburg

Another Virginia town that maintains something of its old-ime flavor is **Fredericksburg**. The town is about a two-our drive from Washington – and roughly half-way to what was the Confederate capital city, Richmond, which explains why four major Civil War battles (Fredericks-urg, Chancellorsville, Spotsylvania, and the Wilderness) vere fought in the vicinity. These are today all part of he ★ **Fredericksburg and Spotsylvania National Mil-tary Park**.

The way to go

In December, 1862, Fredericksburg was the site of one of the bloodiest battles, in which Union General Ambrose E. Burnside ordered his troops across the Rappahanock River and up the steep hill to **Marye's Heights**, only to ee them mowed down again and again by Confederate ire from the parapets at the top of the hill. Burnside's Army of the Potomac lost more than 12,000 men, while he Confederates lost less than half that number.

You can tour these battlefields by car, or walk the nu-nerous trails where you'll find well-preserved trenches nd gunpits. There are also museums and visitors' centers n Fredericksburg and nearby **Chancellorsville**.

First pay a visit to the Visitors' Center at the bottom of Marye's Heights, where an audio-visual presentation ives you a good sense of the troop movements. Then take walk up to the top of Marye's Heights to get a panoramic iew of the countryside below. Up on the hill, along the unken Road, you will see the Confederate trenches which Jnion forces stormed repeatedly without success and at reat loss. In **Fredericksburg National Cemetery**, at the op of the hill, more than 15,000 Union troops are buried.

While in Fredericksburg, cross the Rappahanock River o visit ★ **Chatham** (daily 9am–5pm; closed January 1, December 25), a magnificent Georgian mansion. The uilding served at various times as headquarters for a num-er of Union generals, artillery communications center nd hospital, and is now a museum.

The **James Monroe Museum and Memorial Library**, ituated on land owned by the fifth president, holds a large umber of family pieces, including two Rembrandt Peale

Jefferson,
the third president

portraits of Monroe (daily 9am–5pm; closed January 1, Thanksgiving, December 24–25 & 31). The desk on which he wrote the 1823 Monroe Doctrine, which stated that the United States would oppose any attempt by a European power to establish new colonies in the Americas, can also be seen.

Charlottesville

Charlottesville, Virginia, about 125 miles (200km) from Washington, was the home of Thomas Jefferson, the third president and author of the Declaration of Independence. In 1769, Jefferson built his first hill-top home at ★★★ **Monticello**, 3 miles (5km) southeast of the city (March to October, 8am–5pm; November to February, 9am–4:30pm); an amateur architect, he re-built and altered the building many times over the next 40 years. The end result is an elegant Palladian mansion which has been well preserved and tastefully restored; it still contains many contraptions designed by Jefferson himself, such as a seven-day calendar clock and a device for copying letters by writing with two pens simultaneously.

In town you will find another of Jefferson's architectural creations, the **University of Virginia**. Jefferson founded and designed this university between 1817 and 1826, basing its architectural plan "on the illimitable freedom of the human mind to explore."

The Rotunda – inside and out

Now a UNESCO world heritage site, the historic core of the university centers on the domed **Rotunda**, modeled on the Roman Pantheon. This originally provided space for a laboratory, library, and lecture halls, and its interior has been restored to how it was in Jefferson's time.

Flanking the central green space, called the ★ **Lawn**, is Jefferson's "academical village" in the form of Tuscan colonnades fronting student rooms and pavilions. The pavilions provide faculty residences on the top floor and classrooms on the bottom. Between the pavilions, Jefferson placed 54 Lawn rooms in which students could live, hoping that this arrangement of living and learning spaces would foster a continuous dialogue between students and faculty. In 1826, writer Edgar Allan Poe studied in one of these rooms, until lack of funds forced him to leave. Today the rooms house students who have been recognized by their peers for outstanding service and scholarship.

Skyline Drive

The beautiful Blue Ridge mountains lie just a few hours drive from the nation's capital, 4 miles (6km) east of Luray, Virginia. If you want to make a day of it, start early as it is a long drive and there's much to see. Or, better still, make plans to stay overnight.

Skyline Drive runs through the ★★ **Shenandoah**

…ational Park, a 105-mile (169-km) strip of Blue Ridge …eaks with altitudes up to 4,049ft (1,235m) and hollows …own to 600ft (185m). From the overlooks along the way, …ou'll have a panoramic view of the Shenandoah River …nd the Valley, checked with farms and woodland, and …ith waterfalls and streams flowing through the forests …nd fields. From some of the outlooks, you can see **Mas-nutten** mountain across the valley and the **Allegheny Mountains** in the distance.

The park changes dramatically with the seasons. Many …ildflowers come into bloom during April and May, when …e large-flowered trillium covers the forest floor. Pink …zalea blooms in late May, closely followed by moun-…in laurel in June. Many migrating birds can be seen in …e hills, with the catbird, chestnut-sided warbler, indigo …unting, and towhee in abundance. During the fall there … a brilliance of colors in the park. And during the win-…r, with clear skies and no leaves, you get the best grand …anoramic views.

Pastoral scene on Skyline Drive

Along the route there are a number of visitors' cen-…rs run by the National Park Service. There are also nu-…erous trails running through the forests with adjacent …icnic and camping grounds. At various places in the park …ou'll find both tent and trailer sites with camp stores …nd picnic grounds.

Summer days can be warm, but the nights are cool. Fish-…g is great – the many streams flowing down into the …henandoah are filled with trout. Also, horse-back rid-…g can be enjoyed along the trails.

Some visitors make time to follow the entire Skyline …rive, from Front Royal to Waynesboro, but it is also …orthwhile just to do part of the route. Park headquar-…rs are found at the beginning of the drive at Dickey Ridge …el: (703) 999-2266).

75

The road less traveled

Architecture

Opposite page: St John's, Lafayette Square

Washington's architectural landscape is much more eclectic than one would gather from the bird's eye view of the Mall as seen from Capitol Hill. Although the city's history is rather short – it was decided only in 1790 to site the nation's capital here – the furious pace of building since then has coincided with quite a few changes in architectural fashion, and many beautiful buildings from the 18th, 19th, and 20th centuries have been preserved.

When the District of Columbia was created, there were already two thriving towns in the area, Georgetown and Alexandria. Along their streets you will still find a few Georgian properties, such as the Old Stone House and Carlyle House.

Carlyle House, Alexandria

However, most of the city's important early buildings belong to a form of English neo-Classicism known as Federal, which came into vogue around the time the colonies won independence. Looking to ancient Greece and Rome for inspiration was not only fashionable (Robert Adam's interpretations of Classical form and ornament were all the rage in Britain), but also chimed in with the new republic's democratic ideals. But the Classicism of Pierre L'Enfant's original design for the city was never fully realized. L'Enfant had envisioned grand avenues which would run diagonally across the grid of numbered and lettered streets, and which would end in large open spaces in the form of circles and squares. Many of the avenues were eventually built, and some of the circles – although L'Enfant could never have foreseen the modern-day traffic jams that regularly occur on even the grandest of these avenues.

Although L'Enfant's plans were never followed to the letter, the strict Classicism of the city's monumental core has provided it with its real character. The finest proponent of the Federal style, Benjamin Latrobe, contributed to the design of the Capitol; two of his buildings can also be seen on Lafayette Square: St. John's Church and Decatur House. Other good examples of Federal style can be found in Georgetown, for example on Cox's Row and at Tudor Place.

Old Executive Office Building, and Union Station

After the Civil War, American architecture looked to France rather than England. The Second Empire style, a heavily ornamented style which borrowed from many different periods and used wrought iron to great decorative effect, became popular; the Old Executive Office Building, next to the White House, is a prime example.

Second Empire was followed by Beaux Arts, which is represented by Daniel Burnham's design for Union Station (1908), and Henry Hardenburgh's magnificent Willard Hotel (1901).

"The City of Magnificent Distances"

That Washington has not become a forest of skyscrapers is thanks to zoning restrictions which limit any building in the District from being higher than the Capitol. To see what the city might have looked like without these restrictions, gaze across at Rosslyn, Virginia from Georgetown's Key Bridge. Had such construction been the norm in the District, the monumental city might well have disappeared from the skyline in the frenetic attempt to create needed office space.

The latest development plans of the National Capital Planning Commission propose the development of the extensions of the Capitol to the north along North Capitol Street, and to the south along South Capitol, and to the East along East Capitol all the way to the Anacostia River. This would eliminate the unsightly freeway overpasses and railroad tracks in existence today, and extend the broad avenues of the monumental core of the city along the other "spokes" of the wheel whose center is the Capitol. Government spending restrictions prevent such sweeping plans from being realized any time soon – but the fact that they are on the drawing board provides a strong counterweight to any further deterioration of the inner city.

Another benefit of Washington's enlightened city planning is that many builders, eager to maintain a more traditional building style in the more commercial districts, have renovated some of the older, more elegant office buildings, and, in some cases, built new office buildings in the old style. These are, of course, interspersed with numerous examples of contemporary architectural taste, such as the Kennedy Center (Edward Durell Stone, 1971) and the East Wing of the National Gallery (I.M. Pei, 1978).

I.M. Pei's East Wing

These and other recent buildings, like the Rayburn House Office Building and the new Ronald Reagan Building, have only enhanced the monumental nature of the nation's capital.

Sports

Baseball

Although both of Washington's baseball teams moved to other cities years ago, fans haven't been totally deprived – many have adopted the nearby Baltimore Orioles (tel: (202) 296-2473) as a substitute team. There is easy access to the Orioles' Camden yards, with the MARC train from Washington's Union Station making a stop at the ballpark.

Basketball

For basketball fans there are a number of options. The National Basketball Association's Washington Bullets (tel: (301) 622-3865) play their home games at the U.S. Air Arena in suburban Landover, Maryland, as do Georgetown University's Hoyas. The Bullets will, however, be moving to the new MCI Center near Chinatown when it is completed.

Football

Many Washingtonians may still lament the fact that they no longer have a professional baseball team, but they have transferred their enthusiasm to Washington's professional football team, the Washington Redskins. Every home turf game arouses tremendous civic loyalty.

Redskins fan

The new Jack Kent Cook Stadium (named after the team's colorful owner) is in suburban Maryland. Tickets are always sold out months in advance (tel: (202) 546-2222); ticket-scalpers will be happy to provide you with tickets, but at exorbitant prices. Another option is to check the *Washington Post* classified advertisements section under "Tickets".

Hockey

The local team is the Washington Capitals (tel: (202) 432-7328). They presently play at the U.S. Air Arena, but will also be moving to MCI Center in Chinatown.

Soccer

A more recent addition to the sports arena has been the soccer team, DC United (tel: (703) 478-6600). Soccer has had a difficult time asserting itself in the United States against the more traditional American football, but is rapidly gaining in popularity. DC United plays at RFK Stadium, due east of the Capitol.

*Tomb of the Unknowns,
Arlington National Cemetery*

Capitol in spring

Events Calendar

Mid-February Annual Washington Boat Show. Washington Convention Center, 900 9th Street, N.W.

Mid-March to mid-April Spring Flower Show, U.S. Botanic Garden, Maryland & 1st Streets, S.W.

March 17 St. Patrick's Day Parade. March up Constitution Avenue, N.W. Starts at noon with dancers, bands, bagpipes, and floats.

End of March to mid-April Cherry Blossom Festival. More than 6,000 Japanese cherry trees bloom. National Cherry Blossom Parade, along Constitution Avenue from 7th to 17th Streets. Tel: (202) 728-1137.

Easter White House Easter Egg Roll. Children aged 3 to 6 gather with parents on the South Lawn to roll eggs.

Mid-April White House Spring Garden Tours. A stroll through the Jacqueline Kennedy Rose Gardens and the West Lawn gardens.

Early May Washington National Cathedral Annual Flower Mart, Massachusetts & Wisconsin Avenues. Features flower booths, entertainment, and decorating demonstrations.

Late May Memorial Day Ceremonies. President lays a wreath at the Tomb of the Unknowns in Arlington National Cemetery.

Late May Memorial Day Weekend Concerts, East Lawn of the Capitol. 8pm.

Late May International Gem and Jewelry Show. Washington Convention Center, 900 9th Street, N.W.

June Marine Band's Summer Concert Series, Wednesdays at 8pm at the Capitol and Sundays at 8pm at Sylvan Theater near the Washington Monument.

Late June Festival of American Folklife, National Mall. Arts, crafts, food, and fun.

July 4 Independence Day Celebrations. All-day events on the Mall from 10am. Parade at noon down Constitution Avenue. National Symphony Orchestra performs at 8pm on the west steps of the Capitol. At 9:20pm, fireworks begin on the Mall.

Late August National Frisbee Festival, Washington Monument Grounds, noon–5pm.

Early September Labor Day Concert, National Symphony Orchestra, U.S. Capitol, 8pm.

Early September Kennedy Center Open House. Free concerts and performances, noon–6pm.

Mid-October Taste of DC, popular annual outdoor festival, Downtown.

Mid-October Columbus Day Ceremonies. Columbus Memorial Plaza in front of Union Station.

Columbus statue at Union Station

Mid-October White House Fall Garden & House Tours. Visit the gardens and the famous Rose Garden. Tel: (202) 456 2200.

Mid-November Veterans' Day Ceremonies Arlington National Cemetery, 11am. Presidential wreath-laying at the Tomb of the Unknowns.

Mid-December to early January Christmas Poinsettia Show, U.S. Botanic Garden, 100 Maryland Avenue, S.W.

Late December National Christmas Tree Lighting Pageant of Peace, the Ellipse.

Late December White House Christmas Candlelight Tours. Evening tours of the White House Christmas decorations. Arrive early to avoid long lines.

Food and Drink

Washington is a very cosmopolitan town, so, whatever your tastes, with a little exploration you can almost always find a restaurant that will satisfy you. To find any restaurant at all, you must leave the Mall area, where there are only hot dog stands and the museum cafeterias.

A good area for restaurants is Dupont Circle, which has a wide variety of ethnic cuisines. Adams-Morgan has also become a hot district for dining over the last few years, especially for Spanish and Latin American food. And at Connecticut Avenue and Calvert Street, you'll find an entire block of ethnic restaurants. Chinatown is small, but has some of the best Chinese restaurants in the city.

Harbor terrace

Apart from its shopping, Georgetown is known for its fine restaurants, with an almost infinite variety within a very confined area, from the more upscale spots to run-of-the-mill Irish saloons or British pubs.

Another area that prides itself on its culinary culture is Bethesda, Maryland, only a 20-minute ride from downtown on Metrorail's Red Line. Across the Potomac River in Virginia, there is also a good selection of places to eat. In Alexandria there are scores of interesting restaurants, some located in historic buildings. In Arlington, an area along Wilson Road is now known as "little Saigon" for its Vietnamese, Thai, Cambodian, and other restaurants. There is easy access to most of these from the Clarendon Metrorail stop, on the Orange Line. Rosslyn, two stops earlier, also has a selection of nice restaurants.

8

Tips of at least 15 percent are expected and are generally not included in the bill; check the bill before paying. You can include the tip with the bill if you pay by credit card or leave it separately in cash on the table. Most restaurants are divided into smoking and non-smoking sections. Reserving a table is always recommended.

Outdoor eating, downtown

Restaurant selection

$$$ expensive ($25 or more per person); $$ moderate ($15–25 per person); $ inexpensive (under $15 per person). Prices do not include wine, tax, or gratuities.

The Bombay Club, 815 Connecticut Avenue, N.W., tel: (202) 659-3727. Fancy Indian restaurant, a block from the White House; moderate prices. $$

The Brickskeller, 1523 22nd Street, N.W., tel: (202) 293-1885. Renowned brick-lined basement saloon serving what is claimed to be the "world's largest selection of beer." Good food upstairs. $

Chart House, 1 Cameron Street, Alexandria, Virginia, tel: (703) 684-5080. Located right on the water in the Alexandria Torpedo Factory. $$

Italian delicacies

Good, traditional food

Georgetown Seafood Grill, 3063 M Street, N.W., Georgetown, tel: (202) 333-7038. Nice seafood bar-restaurant, with a variety of grilled fish. $$

Hogate's, 800 Water Street, Waterfront, S.W., tel: (202) 484-6300. Marina restaurant with nautical interior and patio. Full seafood menu, but on the pricey side. $$

Lavandou, 3321 Connecticut Avenue, N.W.; tel: (202) 966-3022, top flight, reasonably priced restaurant with wide array of French dishes. Good wine list. $$

Le Lion d'Or, 1150 Connecticut Avenue, N.W., tel: (202) 296-7972; classic French cooking. One of the city's most expensive places for dinner, but more moderately priced lunch. Reserve in advance and dress smartly. $$$

Les Halles de Paris, 1201 Pennsylvania Avenue, N.W., tel: (202) 347-6848. French country restaurant with excellent food and cigars, and a strong wine/cognac list. $$$

Little Viet Garden, 3012 Wilson Boulevard, Arlington, Virginia, tel: (703) 522-9686. Delicious Vietnamese cuisine in nice, quiet location. Patio dining in summer. $

McCormick & Schmick's Seafood Restaurant, 1652 K Street, N.W., tel: (202) 861-2233. Seattle-based fish restaurant. Good selection, but on the pricey side. $$

Mr. K, 2121 K Street, N.W., tel: (202) 331-8868. A really classy Chinese restaurant downtown, serves a wide range of dishes. $$$

Old Ebbitt Grill, 675 15th Street, tel: (202) 347-4800. Plush re-creation of a 19th-century tavern. Everything from burgers to oysters. $$

Philomena's, 1063 Wisconsin Avenue, N.W., Georgetown, tel: (202) 338-8800. Elegant Italian restaurant near the C&O Canal in Georgetown. Bill Clinton and Helmut Kohl have dined here together. $$$

Seaport Inn, 6 King Street, Alexandria, Virginia, tel: (703) 549-2341. Steak house and seafood restaurant in 18th-century building. $$

Sholl's Colonial Cafeteria, 1990 K Street, N.W., downtown, tel : (202) 293-3065. Self-service café with straightforward menu. A mixed clientele, and during the summer a favorite spot for tourist buses. Can be crowded. $

Taverna The Greek Islands, 307 Pennsylvania Avenue, S.E., tel: (202) 547-8360. Excellent Greek cuisine in a quiet area of town near the Capitol. $$

That's Amore, 5225 Wisconsin Avenue, N.W., tel: (202) 237-7800. Go with a group and enjoy family portions of pasta. Excellent focaccio bread with "Italian butter." $$

Tom Sarris' Orleans House, 1213 Wilson Boulevard, Rosslyn, Virginia, tel: (703) 524-2929. Excellent beef and prime rib amid the decor of a Mississippi river boat. $

Tony Cheng's Mongolian Restaurant, 619 H Street, N.W., Chinatown, tel: (202) 842-8669. Serves both Chinese fare and traditional Mongolian barbecue. $

Shopping

Shopping in the restored Union Station

There are a good number of shopping areas within the city, but these have mainly small shops and boutiques. **Hecht's Department Store** near Metro Center subway station is one of the few department stores that remain downtown. Downtown shopping malls are located at **National Place** (1100 Pennsylvania Avenue, N.W.) and **Union Station**. There are mega-malls in suburban Maryland and Virginia; you can only reach these by car, however.

All of Washington's museums, particularly the **Smithsonian** museums, have well-stocked shops and are good sources for unusual gifts. The biggest one is at the **National Museum of American History**, 14th Street and Constitution Avenue, N.W. There is good shopping in **Georgetown**, on both M Street and Wisconsin Avenue. If you are **downtown**, try the area bordered by I Street, 15th Street, M Street, and 20th Street, N.W. Further north, there is good shopping on Connecticut Avenue around **Dupont Circle** and into **Adams-Morgan**. Across the Potomac, **Alexandria's King Street** has fine shops.

Some of the best book stores are **Barnes & Noble**, 3040 M Street, N.W., Georgetown; **Borders Books & Music**, 1801 K Street, N.W.; **Chapters**, 1512 K Street, N.W.; **Crown Books**, 11 Dupont Circle, N.W. For political memorabilia, from bumper stickers to books and videos, go to **Political Americana** in Union Station. **Tower Records**, 2000 Pennsylvania Avenue, N.W. is the biggest music store in town, with CDs to suit all tastes.

For the best selection of modern and traditional toys, go to **FAO Schwarz**, 3222 M Street, N.W., Georgetown.

Stores are usually open Monday to Saturday, 10am–7pm. Local sales tax is charged on most purchases, and is not included in the price marked on the item or shelf.

Take home a piece of history

Theater, Music, and Dance

The best way to find out what's going on in the city is to buy the Friday edition of the *Washington Post* and look in the "Weekend" section. The daily *Washington Post* will also list the most important events. Or pick up the very useful free paper, *City Paper*, which you will find at many stores and cafés throughout the city.

Theater

A whole gambit of events are usually on offer in the Kennedy Center's three theaters, Opera House, and Concert Hall. For the opera and the more popular musicals, however, most seats are sold in advance by subscription. Only a few seats are generally available for the day's performance and these go quickly (tel: (202) 467-4600).

Other theaters include:

Arena Stage, 6th Street and Maine Avenue, S.W. near the Waterfront (tel: (202) 488-3300). Three stages.

Warner Theater, 13th and E Streets, N.W. (tel: (202) 783-4000). Post-Broadway productions and concerts.

Shakespeare Theater, 450 7th Street, N.W. (tel: (202) 393-2700). Works by Shakespeare and his contemporaries.

Ford's Theater, 511 10th Street, N.W. (tel: (202) 347-4833). Evening and matinee performances.

National Theater, 1321 E Street, N.W. (tel: (202) 628-6161). Pre- and post-Broadway productions as well as musicals.

Music and dance

For classical music, head for the **Kennedy Center Concert Hall** (tel: (202) 467-4600), home of the Washington National Symphony Orchestra. **Lisner Auditorium** (tel: (202) 994-6800) at George Washington University in Foggy Bottom also stages concert performances of operatic and other works.

During the summer you'll also find numerous open-air concerts, some of which are free. At **Wolf Trap Farm Park** in Virginia, just a 40-minute drive from Washington, there are open-air recitals and concerts, and the Wolf Trap Opera Company performs at least one opera every summer (tel: (703) 255-1860).

Between June and August, the various **armed forces' bands** perform on the East Terrace of the Capitol. At the open-air **Sylvan Theater** just south of the Washington Monument, the Army, Air Force, Navy, and Marine Corps bands perform four nights a week (June to August). During July there are a variety of musical programs in the "sunset serenades" at the **National Zoo**.

The Washington Ballet Company performs classical and contemporary ballet at the Kennedy Center.

Ford's – a theater, not just a museum

Wolf Trap concert in Virginia

Nightlife

Georgetown at night

Washington has a good live music scene with bands of all varieties performing every night. Look at Friday's *Washington Post* in the "Weekend" section, or have a stroll around Georgetown, which has the greatest variety of entertainment for almost all ages. Dupont Circle is also an option. Although a center of gay culture, the streets around the Circle also have many straight bars and saloons.

Dance Clubs

The Bayou, 3135 K Street, N.W; good place for rock bands. **Coeur De Lion**, 926 Massachusetts Avenue, N.W. **Hard Rock Café**, 999 E Street, N.W. **Pier 7**, 650 Water Street, S.W.; live music and dancing on the waterfront.

Jazz Clubs

Blues Alley, 1073 Wisconsin Avenue, N.W.; the nation's oldest continuing jazz supper club. Reservations required. Tel: (202) 337-4141. **Butlers – The Cigar Bar**, Grand Hyatt Washington, 10th & H Streets, N.W.; live jazz.

*One of many good venues
for live music*

Bars

Black Rooster Pub, 1919 L Street, N.W.; dart-shooter's paradise; dancing. **Capitol City Brewing Co.**, 1100 New York Avenue, N.W.; friendly saloon. **The Dubliner**, 520 N. Capitol Street; Irish pub with large Capitol Hill clientele. **Garrett's**, 3003 M Street, N.W.; a favorite Georgetown spot with dancing and music. **Hawk and Dove**, 329 Pennsylvania Avenue, S.E.; traditional Capitol Hill bar and restaurant. **Murphy's**, 2609 24th Street, N.W.; friendly atmosphere with live Irish music nightly.

etting There

y Plane

hree major airports service the Washington, D.C. area:
ational Airport, Dulles Airport, and the Baltimore-Wash-
gton International Airport (BWI). There are shuttle ser-
ces from each of them to the city, and many local hotels
ve their own airport transportation service.

Access to Washington is easiest from National as the
ashington Metrorail subway system goes to the airport.
ational is located right across the Potomac River from
e center of town and can be reached quickly. It handles
imarily "short haul" traffic: only destinations within
250 miles (2,000km). The Metrorail station is between
e Main and Interim Terminals, and trains arrive every
w minutes. The Washington Flyer Express Bus also pro-
des frequent service between National, Dulles, and the
owntown Airport Terminal (15th and K Streets, N.W.).

There are no Metrorail connections directly to Dulles,
ut Washington Flyer Express Buses provide a link be-
ween Dulles and Metrorail. Buses run every half hour. It's
so possible to take a Metro bus directly to nine major
owntown hotels. A Washington Flyer taxi can take you
 any destination in metropolitan Washington and sub-
ban Maryland. A more expensive option is the Wash-
gton Flyer Limousine, which will take you to any
etropolitan Washington destination

From Baltimore-Washington International Airport,
ere are regular Amtrak and MARC trains to Union Sta-
on in on Capitol Hill. Alternatively, an hourly Super-
uttle service will take you to the BWI Airport Shuttle
rminal at 15th and K Streets in downtown.

y Train

ong-distance Amtrak trains arrive and leave from Union
ation on Capitol Hill. This is also the downtown stop for
e MARC trains servicing Maryland.

etting Around

rientation

ashington is constructed around Pierre L'Enfant's sys-
m of streets: starting from the Capitol, streets going
st–west are lettered alphatically (A, B, C, D etc); streets
ing north–south are numbered. What can be confus-
g are avenues, named after states which run diagonally.

Always remember that the city is divided into four quad-
nts, with the Capitol as the center. North Capitol and
outh Capitol streets form the east–west divide, and East
apitol Street and the Mall divide the city north south.

Opposite page:
Union Station

Airplane flying into D.C. **89**

The quadrants are consequently named Northwest, Northeast, Southeast, and Southwest. So "A Street", for example, can mean either A Street, Northeast (N.E.) *or* A Street Southeast (S.E.). Most of the tourist and historic sights are however, in the Northwest quadrant.

Subway

The easiest way to get around is by using the city's subway system, the Metrorail, or simply Metro. There are connections to most of the District of Columbia, except Georgetown, as well as lines going into suburban Maryland and Virginia.

Each Metrorail passenger must buy a farecard before traveling, and use it both to be admitted onto the train platform and to leave the station after your journey. The automatic gates deduct the correct fare from the farecard as you leave. You can buy your farecard from a machine in the station, near the automatic gates; the machines accept coins and bills, and you can put as much money on

Suburban Metrorail stations are mostly above ground

M metro **SYSTEM MAP**

Legend
- Red Line • Glenmont/Shady Grove
- Orange Line • New Carrollton/Vienna
- Blue Line • Addison Road/Franconia-Springfield
- Green Line • Branch Avenue/Greenbelt
- Yellow Line • Huntington/Mt. Vernon Sq-UDC

MARC Commuter Rail — Virginia Railway Express
Parking — Transfer Station
Station in Service — Future Station

No Smoking

No Food or Drinks

No Animals (Except Guide Dogs)

No Audio or Video Devices (Without Earphones)

No Litter or Spitting

No Dangerous or Flammable Materials

the farecard as you like, and use it again and again until the credit on it runs out. Fares vary according to the distance traveled and time of day.

Taxis

Taxis are the surest means of transportation, especially if you're out late or are in areas like Georgetown where there are no Metrorail connections. Book a cab in advance, as it can be difficult at certain hours to get one by phone. Fares are reasonable, especially within the District.

Buses

In areas where there are no Metrorail stations, you can always find a Metrobus bus connection. The buses span the entire metropolitan Washington area and are fairly new and comfortable.

Motorists

Parking can be a problem. There are many parking lots in the downtown area, but very little available in the Mall. A good option is to take your car downtown and park it in a lot, then use the Metrorail to get to the various sights you want to visit.

Metrobus goes to places the Metrorail doesn't

Facts for the Visitor

Tourist information and assistance

Tourist information can be obtained from the Washington, D.C. Convention and Visitors Association, 1212 New York Avenue, N.W.; tel: (202) 789-7000 (open Monday to Friday 9am–5pm). Free brochures can be obtained from the DC Committee to Promote Washington, Suite 222, 1212 New York Avenue; N.W.; tel: (202) 347-2873; open Monday to Friday, 9am–5pm. For other assistance, contact the Travelers Aid Society, tel: (202) 546-3120.

Sightseeing tours

Old Town Trolley (202) 832-9800 (daily, 9am–5:30 pm). These old trolley cars (now refurbished with tires rather than on tracks) take you on a 2¼ hour tour. They run a continuous loop around the city, with 19 stops, covering all the major sights and museums. You can get off the trolley at any stop, and get back on when you like.

Tourmobile (202) 554-5100. The Tourmobile offers narrated tours around the city with 18 stops. Like the Old Town Trolley, you can get on and off as you wish.

DC Ducks (202) 966-DUCK. These amphibious carriers will take you to the Mall and then splash into the Potomac for a 90-minute cruise (March to November, Monday to Friday 10am, 2pm, 4pm; Saturday & Sunday,

Local map along the Mall

hourly 10am–4pm). Tickets are available at 1323 Pennsylvania Avenue, N.W., next to the National Theater.

Gray Line Tours (202) 289-1995. Gray Line offers city bus tours, trolley tours, and black heritage tours, starting from the Gray Line terminal at Union Station.

Spirit Cruises (202) 554-8000. Two-hour river cruises with bar and showbands, three-hour dinner cruises, and narrated cruises to Mount Vernon. Departures from Pier 4 at 6th & Water Street, S.W.

DC Bike Tours (202) 466-4486. Guided group rides through the District. Frequent stops along the route.

You can also rent bikes at Thompson's Boat Center, Virginia Ave and Rock Creek Parkway (March–October).

Guide Service of Washington. (202) 628-2842. Licensed tour guides for groups or individuals.

Capitol Entertainment Services Inc. (202) 636-9203. Three-hour black heritage tours.

DC Foot Tour (703) 461-7364. Customized walking tours around major sights and less-visited neighborhoods.

Museum-goers

Opening times

Museums are generally open daily 10am–5:30pm, though they often have extended hours during the summer season. Smaller museums and a few art galleries close for one day a week, usually on Monday or Tuesday. Most of the monuments near the Mall are open daily 24 hours, though they tend to be staffed only between 8am and midnight.

Museum entrance fees

Most of the museums and sites are free. The private museums, however, sometimes charge an entrance fee.

Taxes

The sales tax in Washington is 10 percent, and is generally not included in the price marked on the goods or on the shelf – it is added to your bill when you pay.

The hotel tax is 13 percent; in addition, there is a $1.50 occupancy tax for each night wherever you stay.

Brownstone bank

Currency and exchange

If you are traveling from outside the United States, it is highly recommended to bring a major credit card, traveler's checks in small denominations of U.S. dollars, and a small amount of dollars in low-denomination notes. Most banks will convert your traveler's checks into cash, but it can be difficult to find a bank that will change foreign currency. Many hotels, restaurants and shops will also take dollar traveler's checks in payment.

Emergencies

Dial 911 for police and fire emergencies.

Handicapped

Washington is a great city for the disabled, since all public buildings as well as the Metrorail system have handicap entrances and elevators. Almost every street corner has dropped curbs. Some Metrobuses now have handicap lifts. For information on the handicap services available, call the Washington, D.C. Convention and Visitors Association, tel: (202) 789-7000.

Medical assistance

Medical help has to be paid for instantly, either in cash or by credit card. Europeans and other non-U.S. citizens are strongly advised to take out medical insurance from leaving home. Some credit cards offer certain levels of medical or other insurance, if you use them to pay for your trip. 24-hour pharmacy: CVS Pharmacy, 14th Street, N.W. at Thomas Circle, tel: (202) 628-0720.

Voltage

110v AC.

Public holidays

New Year's Day (January 1); Martin Luther King Day (3rd Monday in January); President's Day (3rd Monday in February); Memorial Day (last Monday in May); Independence Day (July 4); Labor Day (1st Monday in September); Columbus Day (2nd Monday in October); Veterans' Day (November 11); Thanksgiving Day (fourth Thursday in November); Christmas Day (December 25).

Alcohol

The minimum age for the consumption of alcoholic beverages in the District of Columbia is 21.

Telephone

The area code for the District is 202. If you are calling someone in Northern Virginia (across the Potomac), you must first dial the northern Virginia area code, 703. If you are calling suburban Maryland, you must dial 301. These are, however, charged as local calls.

Visas and passports

A valid passport is required to enter the United States. Visas are required for some nationalities. Vaccinations are not required.

Time zones

Washington is on Eastern Standard Time (Greenwich Mean Time minus five hours). From the first Sunday in April until the last Sunday in October, the clock moves forward one hour for Daylight Savings Time.

93

Telephones are plentiful, and accept coins

Hay-Adams Hotel

The historic Willard

Where to Stay

Most hotels discount their rates on the weekends, and prices generally drop during the months of July and August (when Congress is in recess), as well as in December and January. The prices listed here are for double rooms during peak season.

$$$$ *(double rooms from $300)*

Hay-Adams Hotel, 1 Lafayette Square, N.W., Washington, D.C. 20006, tel: (202) 638-6600 or 1-800-228-9290; fax: 638-3803. **Willard-Intercontinental**, 1401 Pennsylvania Ave., N.W., Washington, D.C. 20004, tel: (202) 628-9100, fax: (202) 637-7307. **Watergate Hotel**, 2650 Virginia Avenue, Washington, D.C. 20037, tel: (202) 965-2300, (800) 424-2736, fax: (202) 337-7915. **Renaissance Mayflower**, 1127 Connecticut Avenue, Washington, D.C. 20036, tel: (202) 776-9158, (800) 544-2220, fax: (202) 776-9184. **Four Seasons Hotel**, 2800 Pennsylvania Avenue, Washington, D.C. 20007, tel: (202) 342-0444, fax: (202) 944-2076. **Washington Hilton and Towers**, 1919 Connecticut Avenue, Washington, D.C. 20009, tel: (202) 483-3000, fax: (202) 232-0438.

$$$ *(double rooms from $160–$300)*

The Carlton, 923 16th Street, N.W., Washington, D.C 20006, tel: (202) 638-2626, fax: (202) 347-1806. **Capitol Hilton**, 1001 16th Street, Washington, D.C. 20004, tel (202) 393-1000, fax: (202) 797-5755. **Westin City Center**, 1400 M Street, N.W., Washington, D.C. 20005, tel (202) 429-1700, fax: (202) 785-0786. **Washington Hilton and Towers**, 1919 Connecticut Avenue, Washington, D.C 20009, tel: (202) 483-3000, fax: (202) 265-8221. **ANA Hotel**, 2401 M Street, N.W., Washington, D.C. 20037, tel (202) 429-2400, fax: (202) 457-5010. **Omni Shoreham** 2500 Calvert Street, Washington, D.C. 20008, tel: (202 234-0700, fax: (202) 332-8134. **Sheraton Washington** 2660 Woodley Road, Washington, D.C. 20008, tel: (202 328-2000, fax: (202) 387-5397. **Washington Hotel**, 51 15th Street, N.W., Washington, D.C. 20004, tel: (202) 638-5900, fax: (202) 638-1595. **Jefferson Hotel**, 1200 16t Street, N.W., Washington, D.C. 20036, tel: (202) 347-2200, fax: (202) 331-7982.

$$ *(double rooms from $100–$160)*

Washington Courtyard By Marriott, 1900 Connectic Avenue, Washington, D.C. 20009, tel: (202) 332-930 fax: (202) 328-7039. **Hotel Lombardy**, 2019 Pennsyvania Avenue, N.W., Washington, D.C. 20006, tel: (202 828-2600, fax: (202) 872-0503. **Quality Hotel Dowi town**, 1315 16th Street, N.W., Washington, D.C. 2003

l: (202) 232-8000, fax: (202) 667-9827. **Connecticut
venue Days Inn**, 4400 Connecticut Avenue, Washing-
n, D.C. 20008, tel: (202) 244-5600, fax: 244-6794.

(double rooms starting under $100)

arrington Hotel, 1100 E Street, N.W., Washington, D.C.
0004, tel: (202) 628-8140, fax: (202) 347-3924. **Howard
ohnson Premiere Hotel**, 2601 Virginia Avenue, Wash-
gton, D.C. 20037, tel: (202) 965-2700, fax: (202) 337-
⁴17. **Embassy Inn**, 1627 16th Street, Washington, D.C.
009, tel: (202) 234-7800, fax: (202) 234-3309. **Holiday
n on the Hill**, 415 New Jersey Avenue, N.W., Wash-
ton, D.C. 20001, tel: (202) 638-1616, fax: (202) 638-
)7.

te Hotels

om $100–$300 a night you can rent a small suite, pro-
ing an extra bed alongside the double; ideal for fami-
. The suites also have a kitchen niche.

Georgetown Dutch Inn, 1075 Thomas Jefferson
eet, Washington, D.C. 20007, tel: (202) 337-0900; fax:
02) 333-6526. **Capitol Hill Suites**, 200 C Street, N.W.,
ashington, D.C. 20003, tel: (202) 543-6000, fax: (202)
57-2608. **State Plaza**, 2117 E Street, N.W., Washington,
.C. 20037, tel: (202) 861-8200, fax: (202) 659-8601.
arlyle Suites, 1731 New Hampshire Avenue, N.W.,
ashington, D.C. 20009, tel: (202) 234-3200, fax: (202)
⁴2-1488. **Embassy Inn**, 1627 16th Street, N.W., Wash-
gton, D.C. 20009, tel: (202) 234-7800, fax: (202) 234-
⁵09.

d and Breakfasts

olumbia Guest House, 2005 Columbia Road, N.W.,
ashington, D.C. 20009, tel: (202) 265-4006. **Capitol
ill Bed & Breakfast**, 210 6th Street SE, Washington,
.C. 20003, tel: (202) 544-3926. **Bed & Breakfast
lexandria**, 819 Prince Street, VA 22314, tel: (202) 683-
59; (800) 725-9511. **Kalorama Guest House at Wood-
y Park**, 2700 Cathedral Avenue, N.W., Washington,
.C. 20008, tel: (202) 328-0860, fax: (202) 319-1262.

r further details on bed & breakfasts in Washington,
ntact Bed & Breakfast In Washington, P.O. Box 12011,
ashington, D.C. 20005, tel: (202) 328-3510, fax: (202)
⁴2-3885. They can also provide you with information re-
rding private homes, guest houses, and small hotels,
all price brackets from economy to luxury.

B&B territory

Index